ROUTLEDGE LIBRARY EDITIONS:
NUCLEAR SECURITY

Volume 15

ARMS IN THE '80S

ARMS IN THE '80S
New Developments in the Global Arms Race

JOHN TURNER
STOCKHOLM INTERNATIONAL PEACE
RESEARCH INSTITUTE

LONDON AND NEW YORK

First published in 1985 by Taylor & Francis Ltd

This edition first published in 2021
by Routledge
2 Park Square, Milton Park, Abingdon, Oxon OX14 4RN

and by Routledge
52 Vanderbilt Avenue, New York, NY 10017

Routledge is an imprint of the Taylor & Francis Group, an informa business

© 1985 Stockholm International Peace Research Institute

All rights reserved. No part of this book may be reprinted or reproduced or utilised in any form or by any electronic, mechanical, or other means, now known or hereafter invented, including photocopying and recording, or in any information storage or retrieval system, without permission in writing from the publishers.

Trademark notice: Product or corporate names may be trademarks or registered trademarks, and are used only for identification and explanation without intent to infringe.

British Library Cataloguing in Publication Data
A catalogue record for this book is available from the British Library

ISBN: 978-0-367-50682-7 (Set)
ISBN: 978-1-00-309763-1 (Set) (ebk)
ISBN: 978-0-367-53308-3 (Volume 15) (hbk)
ISBN: 978-1-00-308137-1 (Volume 15) (ebk)

Publisher's Note
The publisher has gone to great lengths to ensure the quality of this reprint but points out that some imperfections in the original copies may be apparent.

Disclaimer
The publisher has made every effort to trace copyright holders and would welcome correspondence from those they have been unable to trace.

Arms in the '80s
NEW DEVELOPMENTS IN THE GLOBAL ARMS RACE

sipri

Stockholm International Peace Research Institute

SIPRI is an independent institute for research into problems of peace and conflict, especially those of arms control and disarmament. It was established in 1966 to commemorate Sweden's 150 years of unbroken peace.

The institute is financed by the Swedish Parliament. The staff, the Governing Board and the Scientific Council are international.

The Board and Scientific Council are not responsible for the views expressed in the publications of the institute.

Governing Board

Rolf Björnerstedt, Chairman (Sweden)
Egon Bahr (FR Germany)
Francesco Calogero (Italy)
Tim Greve (Norway)
Max Jakobson (Finland)
Karlheinz Lohs (German Democratic Republic)
Emma Rothschild (United Kingdom)
The Director

Director

Frank Blackaby (United Kingdom)

Stockholm International Peace Research Institute
Pipers väg 28, S-171 73 Solna, Sweden
Cable: Peaceresearch Stockholm
Telephone: 08-55 97 00

Arms in the '80s

NEW DEVELOPMENTS IN THE
GLOBAL ARMS RACE

John Turner

and

sipri

Stockholm International Peace Research Institute

Taylor & Francis
London and Philadelphia
1985

UK   Taylor & Francis Ltd, 4 John St, London WC1N 2ET

USA   Taylor & Francis Inc., 242 Cherry St, Philadelphia,
        PA 19106-1906

Copyright © SIPRI 1985

All rights reserved. No part of this publication may be reproduced, stored in a retrieval system, or transmitted, in any form or by any means, electronic, electrostatic, magnetic tape, mechanical, photocopying, recording or otherwise, without the prior permission of the copyright owner and publishers.

British Library Cataloguing in Publication Data
Turner, John, *1949 Oct. 17-*
   Arms in the '80s: new developments in the global arms race.
   1. Arms race
   I. Title   II. Stockholm International Peace Research Institute
   355.8'2   U815

ISBN 0-85066-298-2

Library of Congress Cataloging in Publication Data is available

Front cover photograph by Ira Wymgn/SYGMA
Cover design by Malvern Lumsden
Illustrated by John Blackman
Book design by Chris McLeod
Typesetting by Mathematical Composition Setters Ltd, Ivy Street, Salisbury, UK
Printed in Great Britain by Redwood Burn Ltd, Trowbridge, Wilts.

Preface

The world spends an enormous amount on preparations for war. Year by year, more and more resources go into the military sector. More and more complex weapon systems are devised. Of all research scientists and engineers in the world, more than one in four is working for the military.

Throughout the 40 years since the end of World War II, the technological arms race has continued. Now it is moving faster. The United States leads the way, followed by the Soviet Union. Between them, they possess some 50 000 nuclear warheads—more than enough to destroy the world. They plan to increase the number, to make the weapons more accurate, and to base them on new weapon platforms closer to the borders of the other side.

Some people prefer not to think about these things. Many, however, are becoming increasingly concerned—wondering about the future for themselves and for their children. This book is for those who want to know what is happening. What new missiles are being built? What is happening in outer space? What are the facts about chemical weapons? What progress is being made (if any) in Geneva, Vienna and Stockholm, where the powers are negotiating on these matters?

The Stockholm International Peace Research Institute has been concerned with these matters throughout the 19 years of its existence. It is a neutral institute, neither Eastern nor Western. It has established itself as an impartial authority in the field of armaments, disarmament and arms control. Each year SIPRI publishes a comprehensive Yearbook of World Armaments and Disarmament.

The Yearbook is, however, expensive, with many technical chapters. SIPRI therefore commissioned John Turner to write a more popular account, based on the *SIPRI Yearbook 1985*, of what is happening in the world of armaments and disarmament; John Turner worked in close collaboration with SIPRI's research staff. I commend this book to all those who feel a concern about these central questions of peace and war.

Stockholm   **Frank Blackaby**
April 1985   Director

Author's acknowledgements

I am deeply indebted to the research staff at SIPRI whose work I have drawn on extensively in writing this book, and whose comments and suggestions on the text have been both stimulating and helpful. I am also very grateful for the work of Connie Wall, Pauline Torehall and Gillian Stanbridge. Without them there would have been no book.

Contents

Preface v

Introduction 1

SECTION I

Issues and trends in the arms race 3
The technological imperative 3
Technology and arms control 6
Nuclear expansion 6
The importance of cruise missiles 7
Star Wars 9
Emerging technology 9
World spending on arms—going up 11
The arms trade—going down 13

What hope for disarmament? 16
Current negotiations 16
The superpower talks in Geneva 16
The Conference on Disarmament in Geneva 19
Negotiations on force reductions in Europe 20
The Stockholm Conference 21
Looking forward—the third NPT Review Conference 22
Public opinion—are the politicians listening? 23
Nuclear Winter 25
The anti-nuclear drift 28

SECTION II

Nuclear weapons — 31
US nuclear weapon programmes — 32
Soviet nuclear weapon programmes — 35
The nuclear weapon programmes of other countries — 38
Nuclear sea-launched cruise missiles — 39

Space weapons — 41
ASAT weapons — 42
Star Wars — 45
The implications for arms control — 49

Chemical and biological warfare — 51
Chemical armaments — 51
Chemical weapons in NATO — 52
The Soviet Union and other Warsaw Pact countries — 54
Chemical warfare in 1984 — 55
Biological weapons — 56
Major events during 1984 — 58

World military expenditure and arms production — 59
The USA — 60
The NATO spending pattern — 62
The Soviet Union — 65
China — 66
Other parts of the world — 67

The trade in conventional arms — 69
General trends — 69
The suppliers — 70
The changing pattern of arms trade — 74

Nuclear arms control: hitting a moving target — 77
An end to nuclear arms control? — 77
Superpower image and security — 78
Steps towards nuclear disarmament — 80
Negotiating priorities — 81

SECTION III

Reference material 85
Common abbreviations 86
The world's nuclear forces 88
Nuclear explosions, 1945–84 95
US intelligence comparisons of Soviet and US chemical
  weapon stocks 96
World military spending 1975–84, summary table 97
World military spending: annual rates of change, 1976–84 98
The leading major-weapon exporting countries, 1980–84 99
Exports of major weapons to the Third World, 1975–84 100
Imports of major weapons: by region, 1975–84 101
Multilateral arms control agreements 102
List of parties to 10 multilateral treaties 107

Index 111

World Armaments and Disarmament, SIPRI Yearbook 1985 114

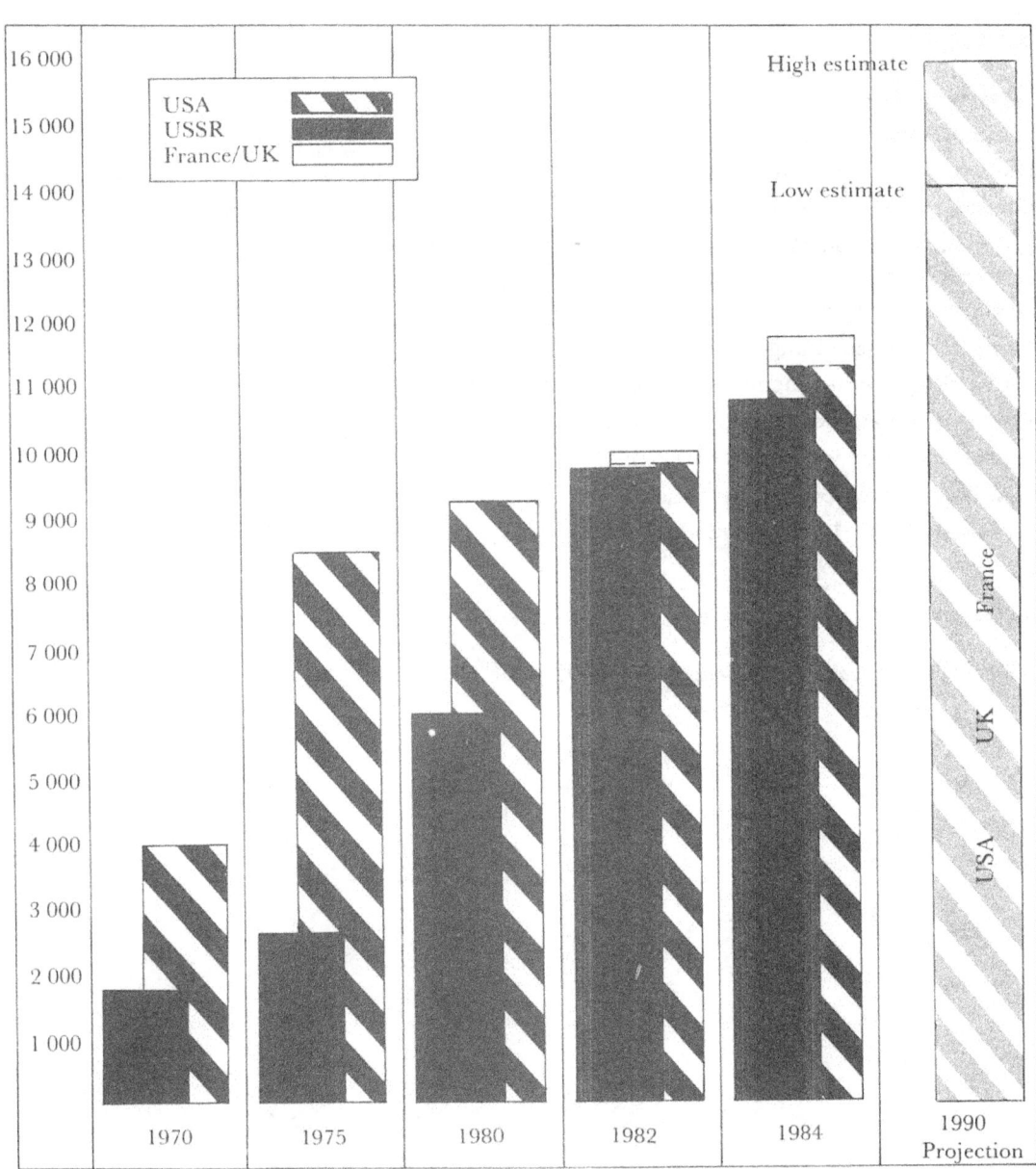

Number of nuclear warheads on strategic and eurostrategic weapons
The graph shows US and Soviet strategic forces, and from 1982 also US, Soviet, French and British eurostrategic missiles. Eurostrategic aircraft are not included. Two things stand out from this graph. First, by 1982 the Soviet Union had achieved broad parity in nuclear warheads with the USA. Second, the projected increase in the warheads held by the USA, France and the UK will almost double the stockpile they had in 1975. Figures for Soviet programmes are not published, but it is unlikely that the Soviet Union will lag behind.
Note: Eurostrategic weapons are those with a range exceeding 1 000 km but less than 5 500 km and targeted on Europe.

Introduction

After the deployment of cruise missiles in Britain and Pershing II missiles in West Germany began at the end of 1983, the Soviet Union walked out of the talks they had been having with the USA in Geneva. During the following year there were no high-level talks between the two superpowers, and in the long-standing multilateral negotiations on arms control in which the superpowers were involved, progress was hardly measurable.

However, as 1984 went on, there were signs of at least some tempering of the language being used by the superpowers with one another. In September, the Soviet Foreign Minister met the US Secretary of State in Washington. They met again in January; and after this meeting it was announced that the two sides would begin talks again in March 1985 in Geneva. These would consider three separate areas under one umbrella: strategic nuclear weapons, intermediate-range nuclear forces, and weapons in space. It is too early to judge how hopeful we may be about these negotiations. They will probably be long and difficult.

The main question is: will the superpowers feel that there is any mutual advantage in placing restrictions on their weapon programmes? The state of public opinion in Europe and the USA may have some influence upon this perception. Although there are signs that the general public is turning against the continuing military build-up, the talks will take place against an unprecedentedly rapid expansion and modernization of nuclear weapon systems. This is a strong signal that the political and military leaders on both sides regard rearmament as providing better chances of security than arms control.

In Section I of this book we look at what has been going on in the arms race; and we report on the minimal progress so far in attempts at controlling it. We examine particularly closely the technological changes in weapon systems. The arms race is very much a race in military technology in which the arsenals, particularly of the superpowers, are constantly being fed with new systems from the laboratories of weapon researchers and the drawing-boards of designers.

On the central issues of the arms race—the militarization of space, new developments in nuclear weapons and changes in nuclear strategy, world spending on arms, the trade in conventional weapons between states and the problem of chemical and biological weapons—there are detailed chapters in the second section of the book.

Section III gives reference material—including statistical tables which support what is written in the text.

Strategic/theatre
Strategic, or intercontinental, weapons have a range of more than 5 500 km. The range of theatre weapons is less than 5 500 km. Theatre nuclear weapons are themselves often divided into long-range (over 1 000 km, such as the so-called eurostrategic weapons), medium-range, and short-range (up to 200 km). Short-range weapons are often referred to as tactical or battlefield nuclear weapons.

SECTION I

Issues and trends in the arms race

The technological imperative

The world stockpile of nuclear weapons continues to increase. Counting all nuclear warheads—strategic, intermediate and tactical—there are probably now about 50 000 nuclear warheads in the armouries of the nuclear weapon powers. On present plans, there could be another 5 000–10 000 warheads added to the world stockpile by the 1990s. That number far exceeds the number of possible targets that could exist in a global nuclear war. It is difficult to conceive of a rational use for the vast numbers of nuclear weapons we now possess, but as each new system is introduced, some rationale is put forward. The developments follow a logic of their own. Some US Navy spokesmen have even justified the widespread deployment of sea-launched cruise missiles (SLCMs) on US ships and submarines as being primarily for use *after* a nuclear war.

It would be wrong to conceive of the arms race as simply a matter of weapon numbers. Technological innovation, especially in the USA, is making great strides forward. This is leading to the introduction of ever more accurate weapons and of new delivery systems for them. Technological competition provides an added impetus to the arms race since new technologies promise new military capabilities. In the area of conventional weapons, so-called emerging technology (ET) offers the possibility of launching highly accurate and selective attacks well behind enemy lines. Other new technologies would use beams of directed energy to destroy enemy forces from space. The arms race arena has already moved beyond the earth into this new frontier.

The constant development of new technologies pushes the arms race onwards. Military men naturally want the latest and best if they can get it. One of the most powerful arguments for getting it is that the other side is working on the same or similar technology. So, it is commonly argued that, "If we don't, they will". Thus there is a constant pressure to develop new systems; and anything new that *can* be done automatically becomes something that *must* be done. New weapon systems are not primarily designed to meet current military needs. Future military needs are

SLCM
Sea-launched cruise missile. It can be fired from surface ships and submarines. It can carry either a conventional warhead or a 200 kt nuclear warhead which it can deliver with an accuracy of around 30 m radius of its target.

ET
Emerging technology. A number of very advanced conventional weapons and means of surveillance and target-seeking. These are now being developed by NATO.

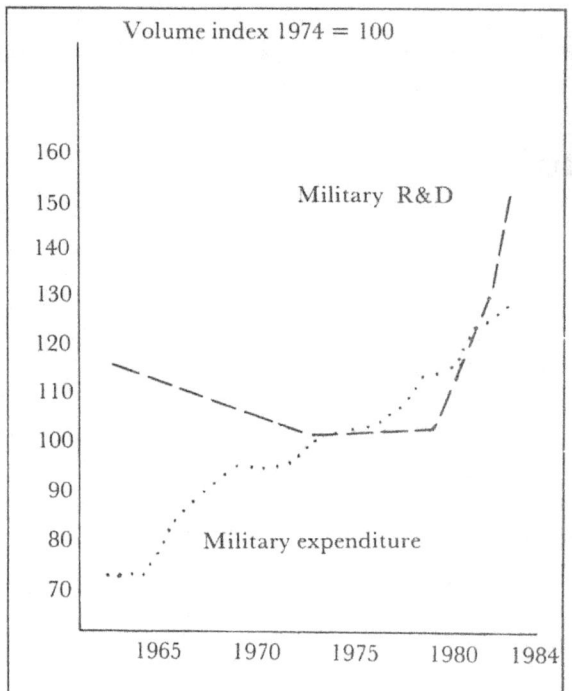 

anticipated. The research and design stages come first, the rationale for deployment comes later. Once a new weapon system has been through lengthy and expensive development and testing it is very difficult *not* to deploy it. Thus, major research and development efforts constitute an almost irresistible pressure for constant technological innovation.

This process, though most visible in the USA, goes on in both superpowers. Each superpower has large numbers of people working in military research. Scientists who have designed a weapon system for possible military use would be out of work if they were not to get down to thinking about the next generation of weapons to follow. The research laboratories, such as Los Alamos and Lawrence Livermore in the USA and their counterparts in the Soviet Union, are vital elements in sustaining the technological imperative, for it is the scientific research which is the first step along the path to eventual deployment. Also, the very fact that research into a particular system is going on in the laboratories of one side raises the spectre that similar research is going on in the laboratories of the other—even if there is no evidence to suggest anything of the kind.

Hence technological improvements may be made and new weapon systems may be developed simply because it has

Military R&D
In the world as a whole, *at least 1 in 4* of all the scientists and engineers working on research and development are working on weapons. World spending on military research and development is rising much faster than military spending as a whole.

Lawrence Livermore Laboratory

become technically possible to do so. Thus, hard on the heels of the development of cruise missiles comes the development of the next generation: faster, more powerful and incorporating 'stealth' technology to make them less visible to radar. Similarly, we have new types of nuclear weapons such as the neutron bomb, the EMP warhead and the X-ray laser. At the design stage, no case needs to be put forward that they are required by the military. They are simply part of the technological development process. There is usually the suggestion that the other side will inevitably develop countermeasures to earlier systems. When, eventually, such countermeasures are indeed developed, they conveniently provide a *post hoc* rationalization for the earlier decision to modernize. But the new system will also face countermeasures. And so the process continues.

New developments by one side certainly do produce innovations to counter them by the other side. If one side develops an accurate homing device for a missile, the other will develop better means of jamming it. Efforts will then be made to try to make the missile less easily detectable. In the nuclear field, attempts by one side to increase the effectiveness of a missile by, say, fitting several warheads on it, may lead to the other side making more of its missiles mobile and therefore harder to target.

Meanwhile, the increasing pace of technological change has also created severe problems for efforts to achieve arms control, for it has undermined traditional methods of assessing the balance of forces on each side.

The Lawrence Livermore Laboratory
This is one of several establishments in the USA which undertake military research. It plays a significant part in the development of nuclear bombs and warheads. Research into and development of new weapon systems are a major feature of the arms race.

EMP
Electromagnetic pulse. This is produced by the interaction of the nuclear radiation of a nuclear explosion and the atoms and molecules of the air. This results in a high-intensity pulse of electromagnetic radiation, which produces very high currents and voltages in cables and metal structures. The result is to burn out the circuits of telephones, TVs, radios and computers. EMP could severely damage command, control, communications and electronic intelligence networks unless they are specially protected from the effects.

Technology and arms control

The arms race can only be halted by constraints on new developments since the competition is as much a matter of technology as one of weapon numbers. Technological change which stresses ever-increased accuracy and faster response to attack is one of the main engines of the arms race. Increases in warhead numbers are only a by-product. This is perhaps why, when arms negotiators discuss "parity" or equality between adversaries in terms of weapon numbers, it is rarely possible to agree.

Because the weapon systems of NATO and the Warsaw Pact are very different, and combinations of them vary so much, it is hard to know what numbers of each would constitute a balance. The agreements reached at the end of the SALT II talks were undermined by lobbies in the USA who argued that the weapon numbers laid down in the SALT II Treaty did not represent parity for the USA, but inferiority. Numerical parity between disparate objects is a slippery concept.

The 'numbers game' is an approach which is unlikely to lead to success. Even if, as occurred with the SALT II Treaty in 1979, some kind of agreement on numbers can be reached, this does nothing to stop technological changes which rapidly undermine those agreements. Thus, a halt to the development and testing of new weapon systems would be the single most effective measure to halt the arms race. Such a move would be the necessary first step along the road to disarmament.

But the 'numbers game' is likely to be a doomed approach for a more fundamental reason: the arms race is an expression of the deep and wide mistrust felt between the world's two major adversaries, the USA and the Soviet Union. It will not be possible to make progress unless attitudes soften so that each side feels able to trust the other's word. As the *SIPRI Yearbook 1984* said: "Security can only be obtained in the long run by policies and practices which increase the feeling of security of both parties. Any step which makes a potential enemy feel more insecure is a backward step, which simply stirs up more trouble for the future. In the long run, security for one side cannot be obtained by deployments which reduce the feeling of security on the other side".

As we point out below in discussing the impact of weapon innovations, recent and planned deployments are likely to have the opposite effect.

Nuclear expansion

The forward plans of the Soviet Union are not published. One of the problems in discussing the policies and capabilities of the Soviet Union is that it is usually necessary to infer them from information supplied by Western, usually US, intelligence agencies. It is therefore often difficult to judge the reliability of that information.

According to US sources the Soviet Union is engaged in the development of 17 new nuclear systems in both strategic and theatre ranges. These include new solid-fuelled missiles to replace the liquid-fuelled models which currently constitute the bulk of the Soviet land-based arsenal. This would enable Soviet missiles to be fired much more quickly than at present. Virtually all US missiles are solid-fuelled.

The Soviet Union is beginning to develop cruise missiles with capabilities that are probably close to those of US missiles, and will probably deploy some of them near to US coastlines. It also has an ambitious programme for building ballistic-missile and cruise-missile carrying submarines. At least one new ICBM and a new SLBM are being tested. These programmes will probably add significantly to the number of warheads deployed by the Soviet Union.

The USA is also in the process of modernizing all three legs of its strategic Triad: land-based, sea-based and air-based nuclear weapons. This programme involves a very large increase in warhead numbers. For example, the MX programme involves the development of a highly accurate ICBM which can carry 10 warheads, each independently targeted, deep into Soviet territory. The MX is designed to hit hardened military targets such as enemy missile silos with very great accuracy.

ICBM
Intercontinental ballistic missile. A ballistic missile with a range of over 5 500 km, thus part of a country's strategic nuclear-weapon arsenal.

SLBM
Submarine-launched ballistic missile.

MX
The MX missile (sometimes known as the 'Peacekeeper') is a large, 4-stage missile which can carry 10–12 independently targetable warheads over a range of 13 000 km and deliver them to within a radius of 130 m of their targets. It is planned to deploy 100 MX missiles by 1989.

The importance of cruise missiles

Another important US development involves cruise missiles. It is planned eventually to deploy some 8 000 of these on ships, submarines and aircraft, and on the ground. They have become a major issue within Europe where they have so far been deployed on ground launchers. But a much bigger programme is under way to fit cruise missiles to B-52 aircraft and to a large range of sea vessels. The cruise missile, with its flexibility and accuracy over great distances, is an ideal weapon to launch from a moving platform. It effectively extends the range of aircraft and ships or submarines which have them, because they can fire at targets far away without themselves becoming vulnerable to attack. Cruise missile deployment in the US Navy will significantly increase the strength and range of US military power in many areas of the globe, including the borders of the Soviet Union.

In Europe, the most worrying deployment is not the ground-launched cruise missile, but the Pershing II in West Germany. The USA claims that it cannot reach Moscow.

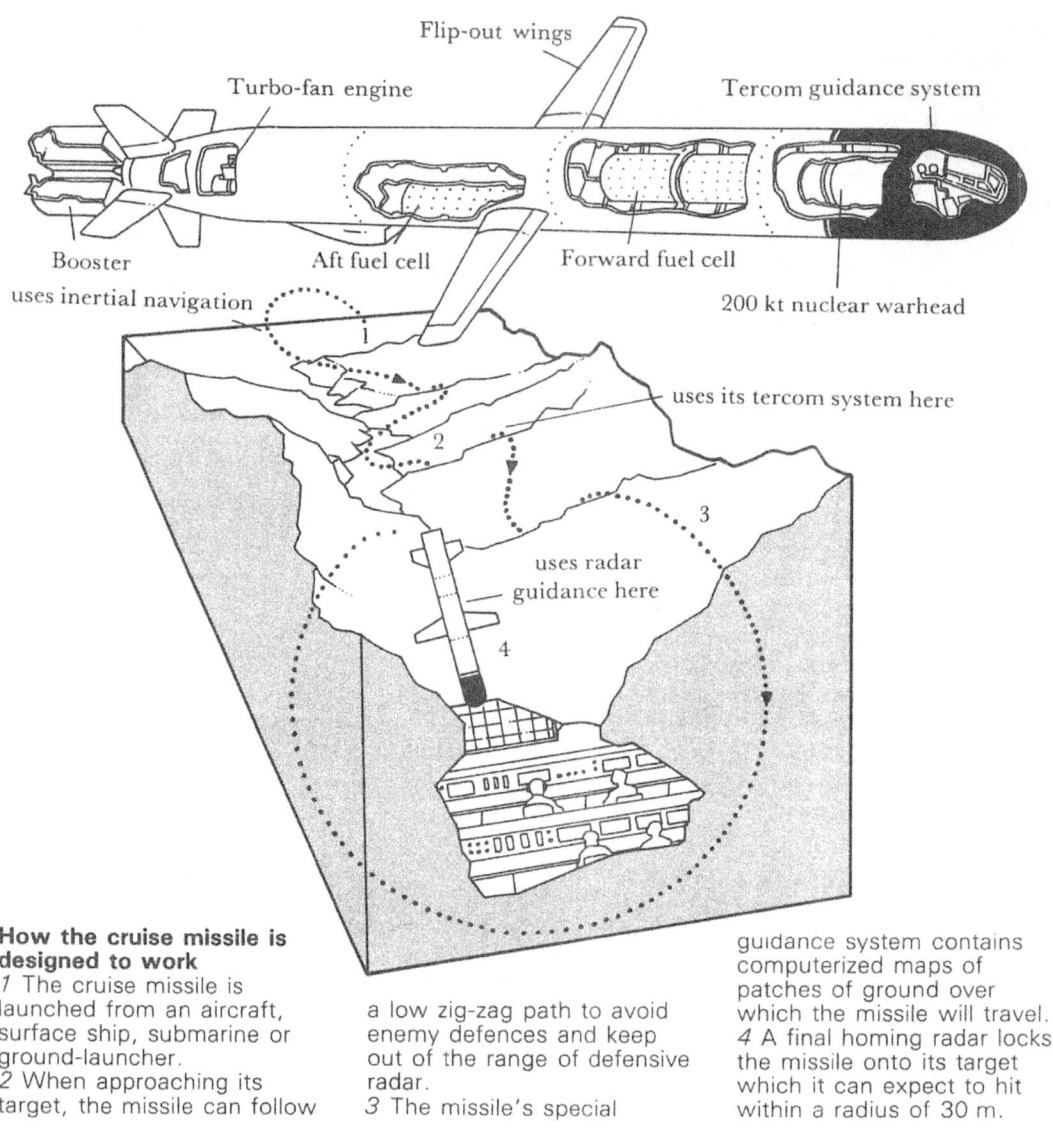

How the cruise missile is designed to work
1 The cruise missile is launched from an aircraft, surface ship, submarine or ground-launcher.
2 When approaching its target, the missile can follow a low zig-zag path to avoid enemy defences and keep out of the range of defensive radar.
3 The missile's special guidance system contains computerized maps of patches of ground over which the missile will travel.
4 A final homing radar locks the missile onto its target which it can expect to hit within a radius of 30 m.

The Soviet Union chooses not to believe this, but instead fears that the Pershings could be used to knock out its command, control, communications and intelligence (C^3I) facilities around Moscow. The deployment of Pershing is therefore destabilizing because it can be seen as a possible first-strike weapon, and because its short flight-time (about 12 minutes) may force the Soviet Union to adopt a launch-on-warning strategy. In other words, the Soviet Union might plan to launch a retaliatory strike (or second strike) immediately on receiving warning that enemy missiles had been launched. This would, of course, be a very dangerous

First-strike
A first-strike weapon is part of an overall capability of destroying within a very short period of time all or nearly all of an adversary's strategic nuclear forces.

development. There would be no time for political intervention that might defuse a developing crisis, little time to think and little time to cross-check for errors. There are enough examples of computers falsely diagnosing an attack to suggest that it is far from impossible that missiles might be launched by mistake.

Star Wars

Perhaps the single most radical development in the nuclear field has been the US proposal for a comprehensive defence screen to protect the United States from ballistic missile attack. The defence establishment in the USA calls it the Strategic Defense Initiative (SDI). It has entered the popular arena under the name 'Star Wars', so called because it envisages using science fiction weapons to create the ultimate defence system: one which offers the possibility, as President Reagan put it, of rendering "nuclear weapons impotent and obsolete".

In reality this is far too bold a claim. The potential of the system cannot, for the foreseeable future, be more than that of an ABM system to defend some land-based ICBMs from attack. It does not replace the present concept of deterrence which relies on the threat of retaliation—inflicting unacceptable damage upon an adversary in response to a nuclear attack. Some of the critics of SDI argue that it may have the opposite effect to that proclaimed by its supporters. Rather than switch the emphasis of deterrence away from offensive weapons and towards defensive systems, it may encourage the Soviet Union to expand its offensive arsenal. We shall consider the arguments in detail in section II of the book. But, whether or not it is a feasible project, SDI has considerable implications for arms control and for the future of negotiations between the USA and the Soviet Union. SDI threatens both to undermine the 1972 ABM Treaty and to open up yet another channel through which the arms race can be pursued, especially on the high-technology front.

Emerging technology

Microtechnology now makes it possible to handle huge quantities of data very quickly. The military applications of this are many: it is possible to detect the movements of enemy forces from afar. These forces can be engaged over great distance, and modern direction-finding missiles can find their targets with great accuracy and speed.
Commanders can send and receive information to and from their own forces very rapidly and thus complex battles over very large areas may be controlled and managed.

Second-strike
A second-strike capability is the ability to survive a nuclear attack and launch a retaliatory strike large enough to inflict intolerable damage on the opponent.

ABM system
Weapon system for intercepting and destroying incoming ballistic missiles.

Technological innovations are thus affecting the shape of conventional warfare and influencing the way in which commanders think about battlefield tactics, especially within the European theatre. New systems, known as emerging technology (ET), are being developed. They consist of highly accurate conventional weapons and efficient methods of surveillance and target seeking. It is hoped that, by increasing the capabilities of conventional weapons, there would be less need to resort to early use of nuclear weapons in a European conflict.

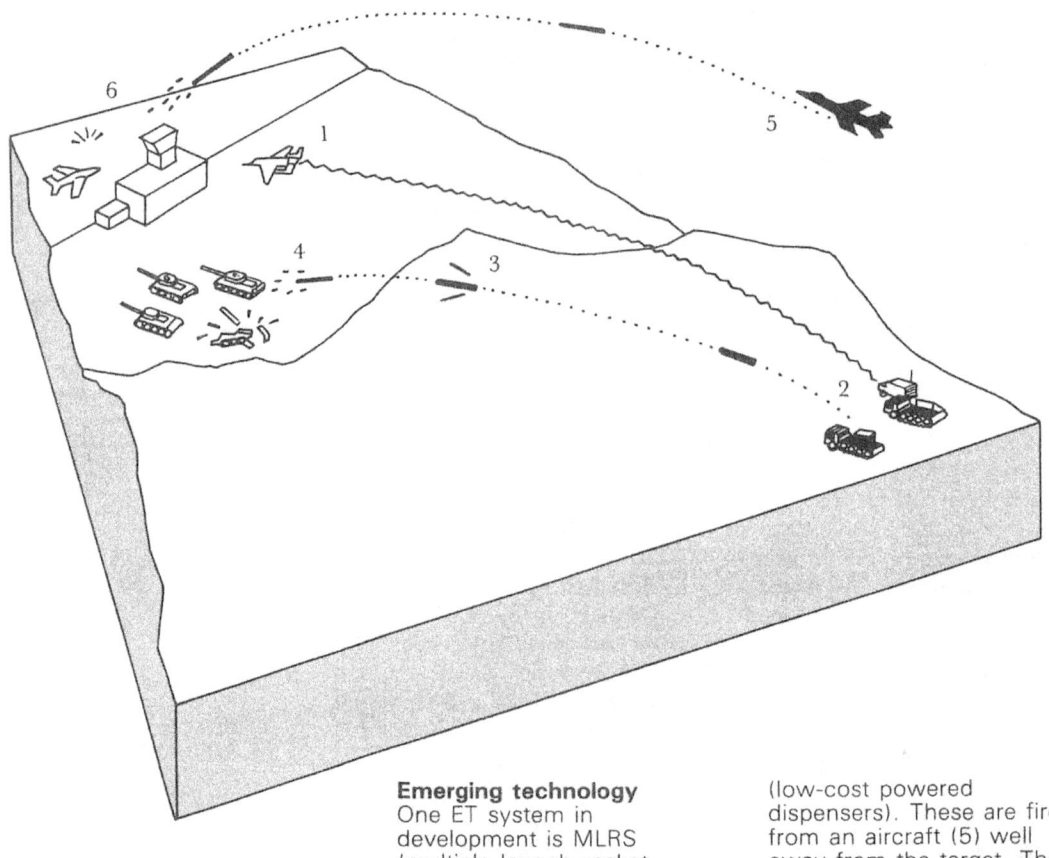

Emerging technology
One ET system in development is MLRS (multiple launch rocket system). A remotely piloted vehicle (1) sends back information about the target area. Rockets (2) are launched. These dispense sub-munitions (3) which then can home in on moving targets using radar guidance (4). Their range is up to 30 km. Fixed targets can be attacked using LOCPODs (low-cost powered dispensers). These are fired from an aircraft (5) well away from the target. They approach using inertial navigation. When in the target area, they dispense large numbers of sub-munitions which can be used, for example, to crater a runway (6). Systems which can strike targets located much deeper within enemy territory are also being planned.

Some of these systems offer the possibility of defending Central Europe against attack by the Warsaw Pact by threatening their follow-on forces. The theory is that, in order to mount a large-scale invasion of Europe, Warsaw Pact forces would have to gather substantial supplies, ammunition and reinforcements behind their front line forces. The new conventional weapons would allow NATO commanders to locate and attack key targets more than 100 km behind the enemy's front lines as well as resisting the main thrust of the attack. If tank concentrations, ammunition supply dumps, bridges and so on could be destroyed early in the fighting, this might be an effective means of weakening or halting the attack.

On the other hand, the technology for these systems is largely untried, expensive and American, so this has led to some caution in Europe. These systems would constitute good targets for a pre-emptive attack from the Warsaw Pact as well as being suitable themselves for such an attack on Warsaw Pact forces. They might therefore have a destabilizing effect. Indeed, the deployment of a form of defence which is likely to be seen as more aggressive may make discussions with the Soviet Union about conventional strengths in Europe and about confidence-building measures that much more difficult. There is another problem—the cost.

New weapon systems are almost always more expensive than those they replace. It is inevitable, therefore, that when countries are involved in extensive modernization programmes, as both the superpowers and several NATO countries are, spending on armaments should be on the increase.

Destabilizing
The deployment of a weapon system can be regarded as destabilizing if, in an international crisis, it might encourage either side to launch a pre-emptive attack, or to launch its weapons for fear that they might be destroyed by an attack. In another sense, something can be said to be destabilizing if it tends to encourage competition in armaments between adversaries.

World spending on arms—going up

World spending on arms continues to rise each year. Recently the rate of increase has speeded up, particularly in the field of military research and development. The expansion of the US military programme has led the increase with an average annual rise of 9.2 per cent during the period 1981–84. The average for the other NATO countries has been 2.5 per cent while the overall Warsaw Pact figure is 2.2 per cent. Without the increases accounted for by the two major alliances, there would probably have been a fall in world spending in 1984. Crippled by debt and by the world recession, many Third World countries have been unable to maintain the levels of spending which they reached in the 1970s. In 1965 the proportion of world arms spending accounted for by the Third World (excluding China) was 6 per cent. This had risen to 20 per cent by 1982, but had fallen back to about 18 per cent by 1984.

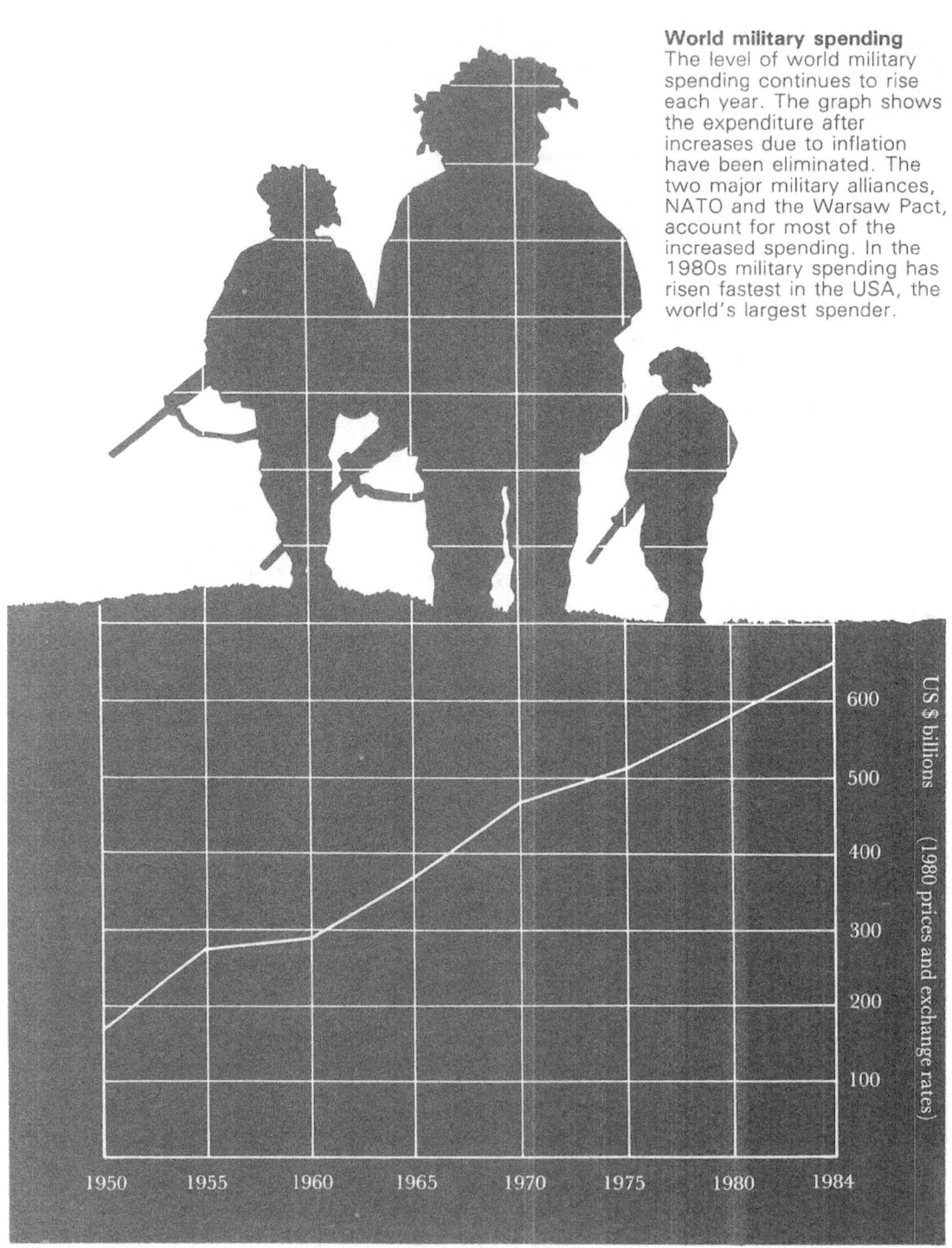

World military spending
The level of world military spending continues to rise each year. The graph shows the expenditure after increases due to inflation have been eliminated. The two major military alliances, NATO and the Warsaw Pact, account for most of the increased spending. In the 1980s military spending has risen fastest in the USA, the world's largest spender.

What has to be remembered about the scale of spending on armaments is that weapons consume resources, both human and monetary, which could be used elsewhere. In a world which is crying out for improvements in health care, education and welfare, and in which there is widespread hunger and even starvation, each dollar spent on arms pushes such improvements further into the future. This is true for both rich and poor nations. The expansion in the US arms budget has been accompanied by savage cuts in health, housing and social welfare programmes.

In the Third World, where the absolute standards of living are, of course, much lower, and therefore the need for improvements in basic living conditions that much more pressing, the impact of military spending is even more devastating. Many Third World nations have been getting poorer in the 1980s. Thus, the living conditions of the majority in those countries have deteriorated. Yet, in two-thirds of these countries, the share of the national income going to the military has either increased or stayed the same. It is a question of priorities: either we spend more of the scarce resources to improve people's living conditions, or we spend more on arms.

The arms trade—going down

Since the beginning of the 1980s the volume of the world arms trade has been declining. This decline has been the result of a number of factors. Most Third World countries, which received 65 per cent of the arms traded in 1984, have been suffering from the world economic recession and from mounting foreign debt. This has reduced their ability to pay. In the 1970s, the major oil-exporting countries invested much of their new-found wealth in extensive weapon purchases. The subsequent decline in the world price of oil in the early 1980s reduced their spending. But many other Third World countries had also invested heavily in weapons in the 1970s and so had no need to make major purchases in the early 1980s. Moreover, an increasing number of Third World countries now have their own arms industries. For example, Indonesia and Egypt now manufacture their own helicopters, while Brazil and South Korea can now make their own tanks. Until the late 1970s they would have had to import these items.

The pattern of the arms trade is changing. There are now more countries trying to sell arms and the market is no longer totally dominated by the superpowers. The European arms producers, in particular, are very aggressive sellers: the cost of producing modern weapon systems is so great that unit costs can only be brought down by selling abroad. But, since the demand for weapons has fallen, arms

Third World
The Third World is the group of less developed countries primarily in the regions of Latin America, Africa and Asia. Japan, whose level of industrialization is higher and is therefore ranked among the industrialized countries, is excluded. Owing to the size of its arms production capability in relation to other Third World countries, China is not included in the Third World in SIPRI statistics.

Imports of major weapons by Third World countries
In the 1970s imports of major weapons by Third World nations went up rapidly, but in the 1980s they have declined sharply, partly because many countries are now fully equipped but mainly because Third World countries have suffered greatly from the world recession.

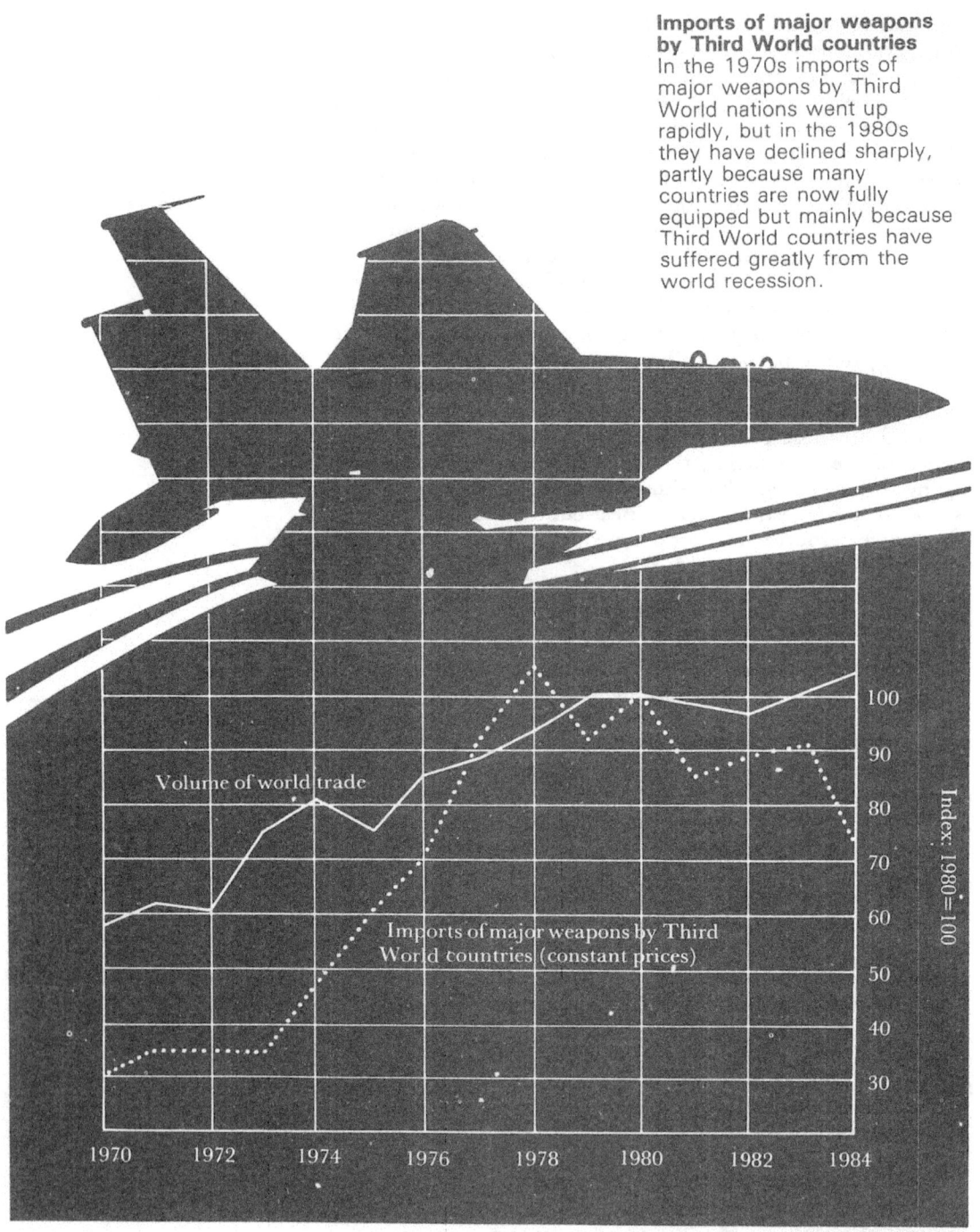

exporting governments and companies are increasingly being compelled to offer attractive deals to potential buyers in order to get contracts. These are not just discounts or credits but also barter deals. The cost to the customer is reduced by the supplier who agrees to take some goods manufactured by the purchasing country in exchange for the arms sales. The governments of exporting countries are willing to subsidize such deals because they are determined to maintain their domestic arms production industries.

It is likely that the arms trade will increase again if world economic conditions improve. The demand will still be there. Weapons are not only used to deter attack but also to wage war. As the Iran–Iraq War shows, arms exporting countries continue to be willing to supply one or even both parties to a conflict. The suppliers will always be anxious to trade their weapons in order to support their domestic arms industries which, they believe, will help to maintain their security.

What hope for disarmament?

Current negotiations

1984 was not a good year for negotiations on controlling armaments. It was a year during which no direct talks between the superpowers took place at a high level. Throughout 1984 the big issues concerning the arms race and the prospects for maintaining peace between nations were not discussed.

However, towards the end of the year it was agreed between the USA and the Soviet Union that they should resume negotiations about the control of nuclear weapons and weapons in space. These talks opened in Geneva in March 1985. One hopes that these talks will have a significant effect upon future developments in the arms race. If successful, they would facilitate a number of regional arms control endeavours. As Andrei Gromyko said in Geneva in January 1985, "The situation in the world as a whole largely depends on the state of US–Soviet relations".

At the present time the planned and deployed weapon systems of the nuclear powers are leading to new and even more dangerous capabilities. If no controls are placed upon these developments the risks of nuclear war may increase massively.

The superpower talks in Geneva

There are three elements in the Geneva talks: strategic nuclear weapons, intermediate-range nuclear weapons and space weapons. The USA apparently takes the line that it might be possible to get a treaty covering one of these areas of negotiation even if no progress has been made on the other two. This is not the Soviet position. The Soviet Union has made it quite clear that it regards an agreement on space weapons as central to the negotiations. Agreements on strategic and intermediate-range nuclear systems are, in the Soviet view, totally dependent on agreement upon space weapons. Given this difference of opinion and the current enthusiasm with which the USA is pursuing SDI, it is likely that the talks will be difficult.

On 13 February 1985 President Reagan told reporters at a press conference that, even if the Soviet Union met US demands to reduce their number of offensive missiles, the USA would continue research into SDI. Two days later a Soviet disarmament official in Geneva stated: "If the

Americans press us to negotiate and [yet still] go ahead with research and elaboration on the so-called star wars, it would certainly torpedo the negotiations".

In previous negotiations on strategic weapons, the USA has concentrated on trying to get the Soviet Union to reduce substantially its land-based ICBM force. This aim reflects US fears that the Soviet Union might use its superior ICBM numbers to devastate the USA's land-based missile forces. It is unlikely that the Soviet Union would accept such a proposal, since the bulk of its nuclear weapon arsenal is land-based, and it is in that area that its technology is most advanced.

It can be argued that the position taken by the USA was an unreal perception of the threat facing it since, as the President's own commission of enquiry into nuclear strategy (the Scowcroft Commission) pointed out, it would be impossible for technical reasons for the Soviet Union to eliminate both the land-based missile sites and the strategic bombing force in a surprise attack. The main reason for this is that the two forces would have to be attacked with different weapons. To hit the bombers before they could take off, the Soviet Union would have to use missiles

launched from submarines stationed close to the US coastline. These would take about 15 minutes to reach their targets. However, they could not be used to attack the land-based missiles because they are not accurate enough. For this purpose the Soviet Union would have to employ its ICBMs. These would take 30 minutes to reach their targets.

Thus, argued the Scowcroft Commission, if the Soviet Union *launched* an attack on both bombers and ICBMs simultaneously, the destruction of the bomber forces would still leave another 15 minutes for the US ICBMs to be launched before the incoming Soviet ICBMs (with their longer flight-times) arrived. If, on the other hand, the Soviet Union planned that both targets should be *hit* simultaneously, the early warning of the launch of the Soviet ICBMs would give the bombers time to take off before they were hit. This would still leave the submarine forces unscathed, since they are invulnerable to a first strike as long as they remain at sea. More than half the US strategic warheads are deployed on submarines.

Towards the end of the last round of negotiations in 1983 the USA put forward the 'build-down' approach in which, for every new warhead introduced, more than one would be withdrawn. It is a proposal which allows modernization but prevents an escalation in numbers.

The Soviet position is likely to be similar to the one it has held for many years: a willingness to have an upper ceiling on warheads or launchers (or both), with some freedom to mix weapon types within these totals.

Then there is the question of the intermediate-range nuclear weapons—those with a range of over 1 000 km but less than 5 500 km. Before the deployment of the first cruise and Pershing II missiles in Europe at the end of 1983, the Soviet Union had offered to retire all of its SS-4s and SS-5s and to reduce the number of its SS-20s targeted on Europe from 243 to about 120, if NATO were prepared to cancel its proposed deployment. It also offered to freeze the number of SS-20s deployed in the eastern part of the Soviet Union as long as the USA did not increase its deployment of nuclear weapons in Asia.

The number proposed by the Soviet Union broadly matched the combined French and British stockpile (which is, of course, targeted on the Soviet Union). The USA wanted to leave these forces out of the equation.

Since the breakdown of the talks, the situation has become more complicated: the deployment of cruise and Pershing II is proceeding, and the Soviet Union has now deployed missiles in Czechoslovakia and East Germany. Further, Western sources say that the Soviet Union has increased the number of SS-20s deployed. The Soviet Union denies this, and has said that it will suspend further deployment up to November 1985. Thus, when the talks resumed, new problems had been added to old ones. Even if the talks stand still, the arms race does not. This is even more true of the third area for discussion.

The Soviet Union has said that, unless there is agreement about space weapons (that is, any weapons aimed at targets in space as well as space-based weapons which can attack targets on Earth), it will not agree to reduce offensive nuclear weapon systems. It has expressed concern over the declared intention of the USA to investigate whether space-based anti-ballistic missile systems can be developed. There will be many problems with this part of the Geneva negotiations. Any agreement on the control of space weapons would have to deal with two separate but related issues—the question of weapons which could attack satellites, and the question of weapons which could shoot down ballistic missiles. However, the technologies for these two purposes have a great deal in common, so that it will not be easy to deal with them separately.

If progress in arms control is likely to be very difficult to achieve during 1985, that would merely be a continuation of the pattern maintained during 1984. Several sets of multilateral talks took place which could have been very important for controlling the arms race. Unfortunately, they too were blighted by the frostiness of the relationships between the USA and the Soviet Union. In 1984, the political will for success was absent, as the negligible achievements of a variety of disarmament discussions testify.

The Conference on Disarmament in Geneva

The Conference on Disarmament has been meeting in Geneva for many years now. A total of 40 nations are represented there. Some progress was made concerning chemical disarmament in 1984. Discussions took place about how to deal with chemicals which could be used for both peaceful and military ends. There was also discussion about the timetable for the destruction of existing chemical weapon stocks and production facilities, which could be a process lasting up to 10 years. The Soviet Union seems to be willing to accept that there should be inspectors from other countries permanently installed at destruction sites. This question of inspection has always been a stumbling-block in negotiations with the Soviet Union.

The USA, however, put forward a draft convention which included proposals for "special inspections" to check for secret stocks of chemical weapons and for any suspected undisclosed production. The inspectors would be able to ask to inspect *any* location or facility owned or controlled by a government. Such a demand for unrestricted access, to make certain that all stocks had been destroyed and that no new chemical warfare agents were being produced, seems to be excessive. It would open up to inspection defence establishments and chemical production plants to a degree no country could realistically be expected to accept. The Soviet Union rejected the US proposals. In February 1985 a Soviet delegate at the Geneva conference announced that there would not be any chemical weapon agreement in 1985 if the USA stuck to its proposals.

The tripartite talks about a Comprehensive Test Ban Treaty (CTBT) involving the USA, the Soviet Union and the UK have been suspended since 1980, when the incoming Reagan Administration declared that, in its view, negotiations on a comprehensive test ban were not a priority.

At the Conference on Disarmament there were no actual negotiations on a CTB during 1984, but the Japanese delegation proposed that the nuclear powers should move towards a complete ban on testing by gradually reducing the maximum yield on underground tests. The current upper limit accepted by the USA and the Soviet Union is 150 kt. The negotiation of a ban on weapon testing is rightly regarded as a very important step towards halting the nuclear arms race because it could stop the constant qualitative improvement of weapon systems. A CTB would make it difficult or even impossible to test the designs of nuclear warheads and bombs. But it is quite clear that neither of the superpowers is prepared, at the moment, to accept a ban on testing *for all time*.

Nor are France or China likely to sign such a treaty. They argue that their nuclear weapon programmes are so far behind those of the superpowers that they must continue to develop them and must therefore continue testing. In these circumstances, perhaps the best one can hope for is a limited programme of meaningful restrictions on testing.

CTBT
A Comprehensive Test Ban Treaty would prohibit the testing of any nuclear warhead in any environment. This would inhibit the modernization of nuclear warheads. The 1963 Partial Test Ban Treaty bans atmospheric testing but does not prevent underground tests.

Negotiations on force reductions in Europe

These talks, which involve all the countries with military forces stationed in Europe, have been continuing now for 12 years in Vienna. They made hardly any progress during 1984. Their aim is to reduce the military forces on both sides. There has been an agreement that the total ground and air force manpower on either side should be reduced to 900 000. But the participants cannot agree on how many Warsaw Pact troops are currently in Central Europe. NATO estimates suggest that the Warsaw Pact number should be some 250 000 higher than the figure which the Warsaw Pact has declared. So there is stalemate. With political will, it should be possible to find a way round this disagreement, but that is just what is lacking.

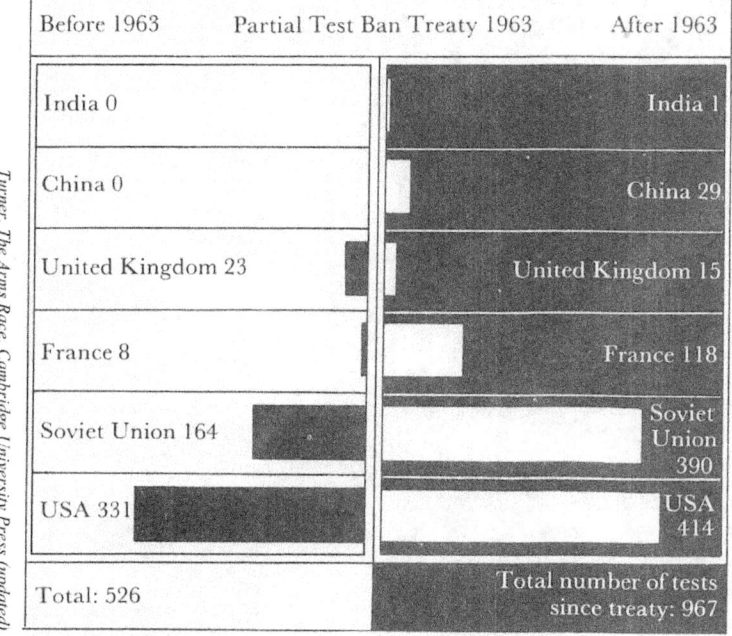

Nuclear explosions since 1945

Between July 1945 and the end of 1984, 1 493 nuclear explosions were carried out. The Partial Test Ban Treaty, signed in 1963, did nothing to reduce the number of tests. Nearly twice as many tests were carried out in the 21 years since 1963 as in the 18 years before. But the treaty did reduce the amount of global nuclear fall-out in the atmosphere. Even here, however, success has not been total. 22 of China's 29 tests and 41 of France's 118 tests since 1963 have been carried out in the atmosphere.

Turner, The Arms Race, Cambridge University Press (updated)

The Stockholm Conference

This conference, which opened in January 1984, also made little progress. It involves the European nations (with the exception of Albania and Andorra) plus Canada and the USA, and is part of the process begun by the 1975 Helsinki Conference on Security and Co-operation in Europe.

The purpose of the conference is not to discuss actual disarmament measures but to prepare the ground for such steps by negotiating measures which would build confidence and enhance security. The primary goal of the Stockholm Conference is to achieve agreements which soothe fears of surprise attack and reduce the chances of countries stumbling into war.

The NATO countries wanted to keep within the mandate which, they argued, the conference had been given—and that was to discuss *military* confidence-building measures. This would include such items as the exchange of information on the structure of ground forces, the prior notification of military exercises and major troop movements, and compulsory invitations to foreign observers to witness such manoeuvres.

The Warsaw Pact delegates put forward, in the first place, a very different set of proposals—such as proposals for an agreement on the non-use of force to settle disputes, an agreement that neither side would be the first to use

The Stockholm Conference
The Stockholm Conference in session in January 1984.

nuclear weapons, and that there should be a chemical weapon-free zone in Europe and nuclear weapon-free zones in the Balkans and northern and central Europe. The NATO side argued that most of these proposals were outside the mandate of the conference and, if they were to be discussed, it should happen elsewhere.

The proposals from the neutral and non-aligned states (Austria, Cyprus, Finland, Liechtenstein, Malta, San Marino, Sweden, Switzerland and Yugoslavia) were nearer to the NATO position, with the added idea of imposing some limits on, for example, the size of military manoeuvres.

The progress that has been made is to set up two working parties: one to tackle the military confidence-building measures, and the other to tackle all the rest. However, it is agreed that, just because an item is being discussed at a conference, it does not necessarily follow that it should have a place in the final document.

Looking forward—the third NPT Review Conference

The third Review Conference of the Non-Proliferation Treaty (NPT) will be held in Geneva in the autumn of 1985. The NPT is a very important treaty. In it, countries without nuclear weapons pledged that they would not acquire them. For their part, the three nuclear weapon powers that signed the treaty—the USA, the Soviet Union and the UK—pledged themselves to help non-nuclear states to make peaceful use of nuclear energy but to impede attempts by non-nuclear weapon powers to obtain nuclear materials for weapons. Further, the nuclear weapon powers pledged themselves to undertake negotiations among themselves for nuclear disarmament.

The treaty has held remarkably well. For more than a decade, since the 1974 Indian nuclear explosion, despite the steady development of nuclear energy in different parts of the world, no country has definitely demonstrated a nuclear weapon capability. A very large number of countries are patries to the treaty. But the treaty is under threat, and the Review Conference will need to address itself to the factors that might undermine it.

There are a small number of countries which have not joined the treaty and which have been carrying out some significant nuclear activities without adequate safeguards (such as the inspection of nuclear installations) to see that no nuclear material is being diverted to make weapons. These countries include Argentina, Brazil, India, Israel, Pakistan and South Africa.

One of the main factors undermining the NPT is the total failure of the nuclear weapon powers to meet their treaty obligations to make progress towards disarmament. This failure undermines the treaty because, by their actions, the nuclear weapon states demonstrate that they find the possession of nuclear weapons politically useful. If the major powers think that nuclear weapons are worth having, why should other states not feel the same way? Unfortunately, it is most unlikely that in the present climate the Review Conference will be able to make many inroads upon these positions. As we argue elsewhere, when there is no hope of an agreed final document, it is probably better not to try for one.

Public opinion—are the politicians listening?

The previous section has detailed the painfully slow progress of arms negotiations between the representatives of nations. Yet there is clear evidence that the general public in the West is keen to see such agreements reached and for nuclear weapons to be brought under control. In the period since the end of World War II, opinion about nuclear weapons has shifted. A survey of opinion polls in the USA shows that there is much less optimism that nuclear weapons can be used to preserve world peace and prevent war. Similarly, there is greater pessimism about the

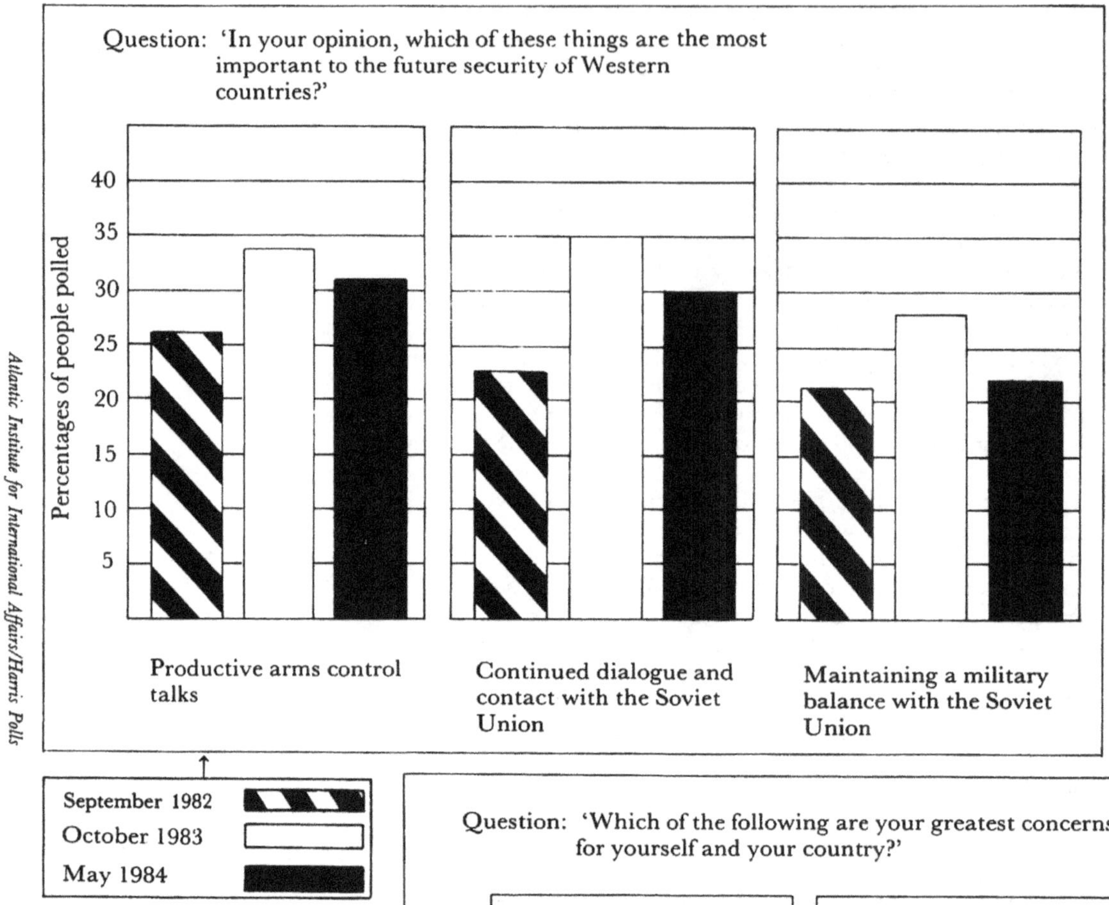

Atlantic Institute for International Affairs/Harris Polls

Question: 'In your opinion, which of these things are the most important to the future security of Western countries?'

[Bar chart showing percentages of people polled for three categories: "Productive arms control talks" (Sept 1982: 26, Oct 1983: 34, May 1984: 31), "Continued dialogue and contact with the Soviet Union" (Sept 1982: 22, Oct 1983: 35, May 1984: 30), "Maintaining a military balance with the Soviet Union" (Sept 1982: 21, Oct 1983: 28, May 1984: 22)]

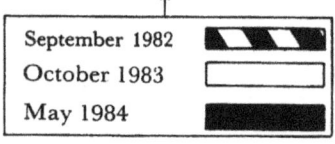

September 1982
October 1983
May 1984

March 1983
October 1983
May 1984

Public opinion on the arms race in nine countries
The graphs show the results of opinion polls taken in West Germany, France, Italy, Japan, the Netherlands, Norway, Spain, the UK and the USA. The graphs are drawn from figures which are averaged, taking into account the population sizes of different countries.

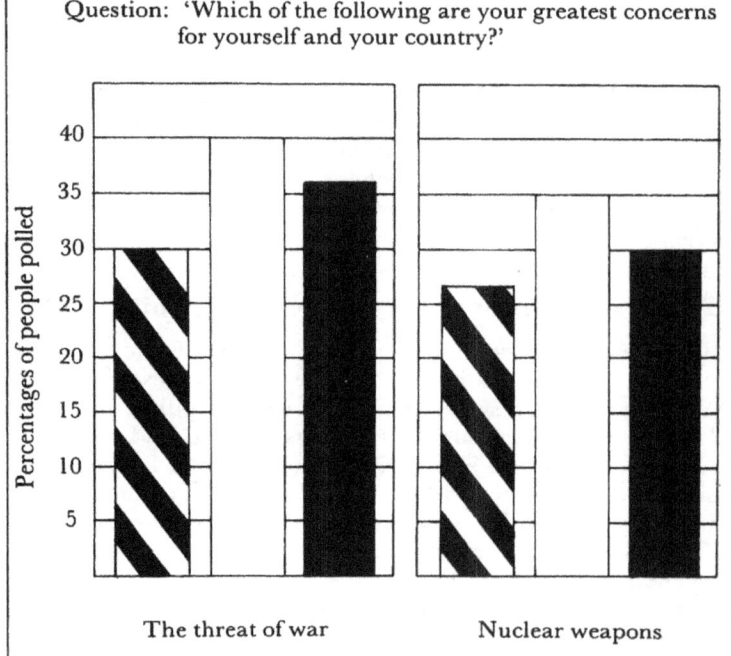

Question: 'Which of the following are your greatest concerns for yourself and your country?'

[Bar chart showing percentages of people polled for "The threat of war" (March 1983: 30, Oct 1983: 40, May 1984: 36) and "Nuclear weapons" (March 1983: 27, Oct 1983: 35, May 1984: 30)]

possibility of survival after a nuclear war. Recent scientific work on the climatic effects of global nuclear war tends to underline such feelings and to strengthen the growing mood, particularly in Europe, that the very existence of nuclear weapons is a moral outrage.

Nuclear Winter

At the end of 1983 new suggestions emerged from a number of scientists working in both the USA and the Soviet Union about the long-term effects of global nuclear war. Prior to the appearance of this work, it was believed that, while many millions of people would die from the prompt and delayed effects of the war (if not from the initial blast, heat or gamma rays, then from fall-out, disease and so forth), nevertheless ultimate recovery would be possible. The devastation of much of the northern hemisphere would be catastrophic, but it was believed that reconstruction of shattered societies would eventually take place. This process could be speeded up if help came from the relatively unscathed countries of the northern and southern hemispheres.

The Nuclear Winter research challenges these assumptions. If the predictions of these scientists are correct, a nuclear war would radically alter the world's climate for up to a few months by producing a dense cloud of dust and smoke which would rapidly encircle the northern hemisphere. This would cut out perhaps 90–99 per cent of the sun's energy for a week or so, thereby reducing surface temperatures dramatically. Temperatures in the northern hemisphere are predicted to drop by between 15°C and 30°C. These temperatures would persist for several weeks and then gradually revert to essentially normal over a period of months. As the layer of smoke and dust gradually thinned, dangerously high doses of ultraviolet radiation would penetrate the depleted ozone layer above the earth. Not only would people die directly from the cold, but the northern hemisphere's ecosystems would be seriously damaged. Crops, trees, other plants and animals, and even plankton, on which all ocean life depends, would be destroyed in part by the effects of the Nuclear Winter.

The models which predict the effects of the Nuclear Winter only apply to the northern hemisphere, but it has been suggested that the consequences might not be confined to this region. The dense shroud of smoke and dust in the northern hemisphere could be expected to cause major changes in the earth's wind systems. The cloud might conceivably move southwards to smother the tropics and much of the southern hemisphere. The catastrophe would thus be global. No one would escape.

Making the Nuclear Winter

The predictions of the Nuclear Winter models

The intense heat from nuclear explosions sets fire to cities, fuel stores and areas of forest. Massive quantities of dust and smoke (soot) are sucked up into the atmosphere.

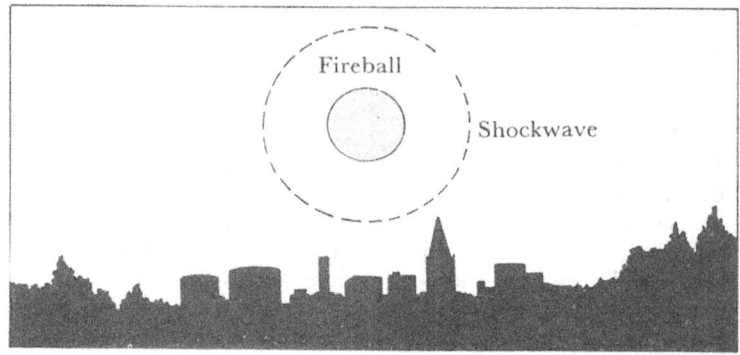

The fires started by the nuclear explosions spread and send further quantities of smoke into the atmosphere.

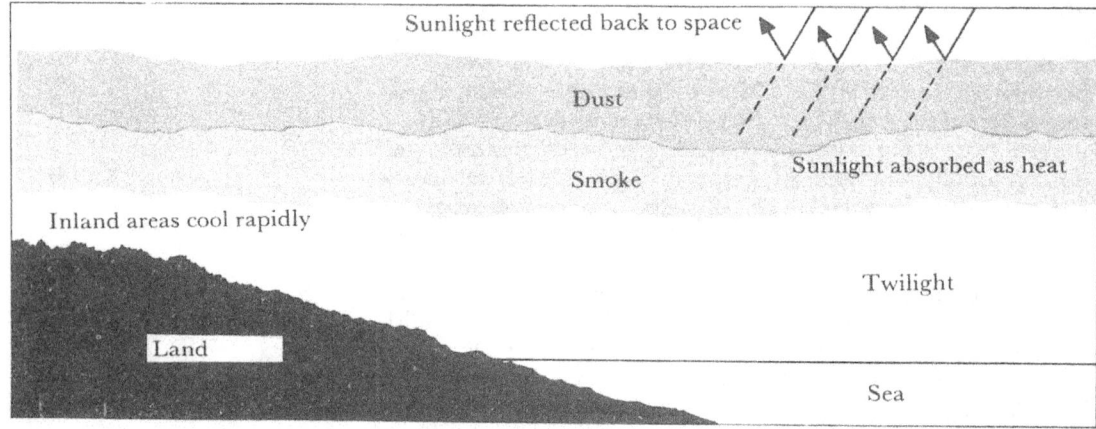

Within days a dense blanket of smoke and dust shrouds the northern hemisphere. This blots out nearly all of the light from the sun, which is absorbed as heat by the cloud or reflected back from the cloud into space. Beneath the cloud there is virtual darkness for a few days. But more importantly, without the warming effect of the sun, the inland areas of the earth's surface cool rapidly.

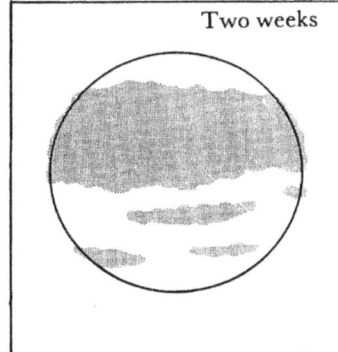

Two weeks

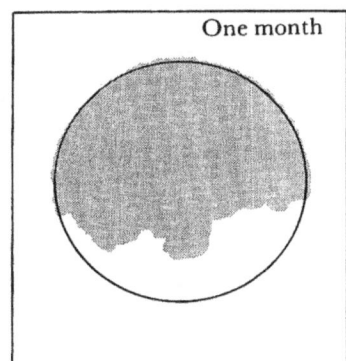

One month

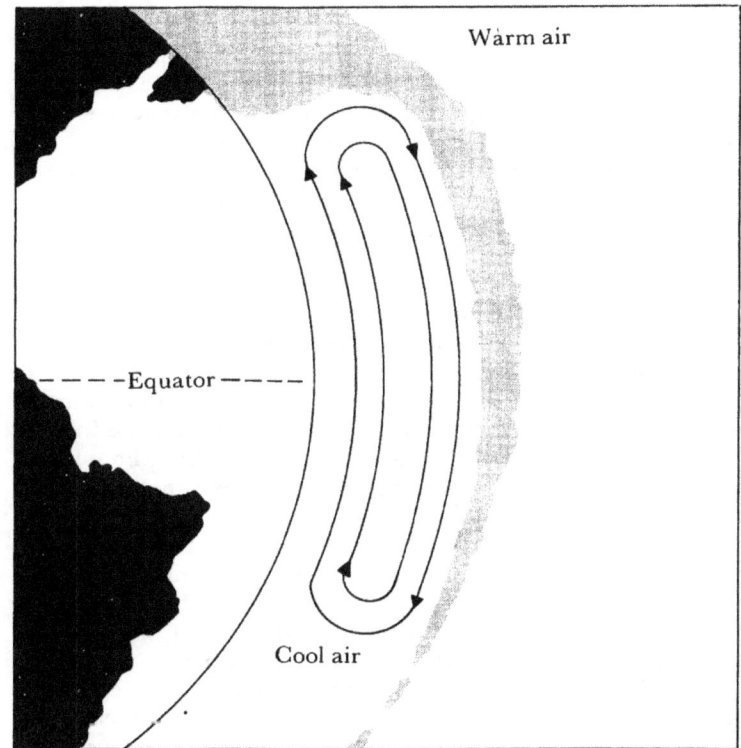

In time the weather system of the entire planet may be affected. Air currents may be set up which move the clouds southwards. Within a month, the blanket, now much thinner, may cover much of the earth's surface. The cold of the Nuclear Winter persists for several months.

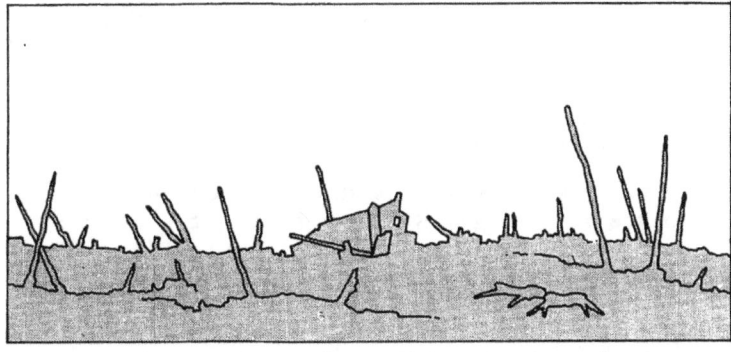

The lack of warmth is catastrophic for many forms of life. No food can be grown on the frozen wastelands of the northern hemisphere. Tropical forests may be destroyed by the low temperatures. Food chains in the oceans might be disrupted. People and animals starve or succumb to disease.

The predictions are, of course, based on computer models, but they have received considerable support from a number of other scientists in both the East and the West. It is worth noting that one of the models predicts that the Nuclear Winter would result not just from a nuclear exchange in the region of 5 000 megatons (that is, one in which a substantial part of the arsenals of the superpowers is unleashed), but the same result would follow from an exchange of as little as 100 Mt if the attack were concentrated upon cities.

There are considerable uncertainties about the predictions of the Nuclear Winter models. They are theoretical models which have to be based upon a wide range of assumptions about, for example, the degree to which forests would burn and thus the amount of smoke that would be propelled into the atmosphere. There are uncertainties too about how long the smoke particles would remain in the atmosphere before being washed out by rainfall. Further, the temperature drop predicted by the models could be significantly reduced by the capacity of the oceans to retain heat, certainly so near such bodies of water. Since these cover nearly four-fifths of the earth's surface, this adds yet another area of uncertainty into the Nuclear Winter predictions.

But, despite the uncertainties, there seems to be general agreement that there would be significant climatic effects resulting from a major nuclear war. The degree of severity and distribution of these effects around the globe remain disputed or undefined. Further research needs to be undertaken to produce more reliable predictions. For if it were to turn out that the life-threatening consequences of nuclear war would affect all participants in the fighting as well as other countries not involved, then the implications for deterrence and for the credibility of policies which are based on a threat to use nuclear weapons would be great indeed.

The anti-nuclear drift

In the southern hemisphere, Australia has refused to take part in the monitoring of MX tests for the USA; and New Zealand (as well as China and Iceland) has refused to allow US naval vessels to use its ports since the USA will not say whether they carry nuclear weapons. In November 1984 member countries of the South Pacific Forum (including Australia, New Zealand, Fiji and Papua New Guinea) prepared a draft treaty on a nuclear weapon-free zone in the South Pacific which will be considered by the relevant heads of government in 1985.

In Western Europe, although there have been fewer anti-nuclear mass demonstrations, public opinion polls do not suggest any weakening of the opposition to the deployment of new US missiles in Europe. Opinion polls taken in the UK, West Germany, the Netherlands, Belgium and Italy show clear majorities against those deployments.

Furthermore, in opinion polls carried out in nine countries, there was a clear preference expressed for dialogue and contact with the Soviet Union; this was considered more important than maintaining a military balance. In the USA, a survey of public opinion polls undertaken before the Presidential elections showed that there had been a dramatic shift in public attitudes towards nuclear weapons in the post-war period. In 1949 only 29 per cent of the population thought that the invention of the atomic bomb had been a bad thing; by 1982 that figure had grown to 65 per cent. The survey went on to suggest that its findings, if extrapolated across the entire US population, would show that about three-quarters of Americans believed that nuclear war would be suicidal, that both superpowers have an 'overkill' capacity, and that a nuclear arms race could not be won.

Opinion surveys in the West tend to show that, while people do regard the Soviet Union as a dangerous adversary, they do not in general believe that the differences can best be solved by confrontation and through the continuation of the arms race. Military and political leaders who put obstacles in the way of meaningful negotiations are not expressing the true wishes of the electorate.

SECTION II

Nuclear weapons

Introduction

The nuclear arms race has intensified in the 1980s. The world stockpile of nuclear weapons has now reached about 50 000 warheads. Recent additions and planned deployments will add thousands more warheads to the existing stocks within the next few years. In 1984 the USA alone added 800 new warheads to its strategic stockpile. In placing MIRVs on its ICBM force, the Soviet Union has increased its strategic warheads by 400 per cent since the late 1970s.

But it is not just a question of warhead numbers. There are two particularly dangerous developments. First, the increasing accuracy with which nuclear weapons can be directed to their targets has meant that new weapons are more suited for attacking the military targets of the enemy than those they have replaced. Second, there is an increasing tendency for the superpowers to deploy these weapons in forward positions. For example the Pershing II missile has been deployed in West Germany and the SS-12 and -22 in East Germany and Czechoslovakia. Cruise missiles are also being deployed in forward positions—US one's in the North Atlantic and Soviet ones close to US coastlines.

These two factors combine to produce a stance which is aggressive and provocative because it can be seen by the other side as a preparation for striking first. In any case, in a crisis where the flight time of incoming missiles aimed at one's military positions can be as little as 12 minutes there is very little thinking time and a temptation to fire first, or at least early in any conflict, on the principle that one must either "use 'em or lose 'em". These developments thus heighten the danger of rapid escalation to all-out war in a crisis.

New roles are being planned for nuclear weapons as technological developments enable planners to think of using highly sophisticated weapons in selective ways. The introduction of new sea-launched cruise missiles will change the role of the navy in wartime. The proposed ballistic-missile defence system, known as 'Star Wars' or SDI, will be integrated into overall war-fighting plans—plans that actually envisage fighting and 'prevailing' in a nuclear war. These developments heighten the sense of inferiority already felt by the Soviet Union. It is therefore likely to worsen the

MIRV
Multiple independently targetable re-entry vehicle. One of the major developments in the nuclear arms race in the 1970s was the practice of placing more than one warhead on a missile. Advances in computer technology have made it possible to guide each re-entry vehicle, and the warhead it carries, to a separate target.

prospects for reaching any kind of arms control agreement in the near future.

The Soviet Union too continues to modernize its nuclear forces. This reinforces the threats perceived by the USA. New developments in nuclear weapons in 1984 were therefore of major importance. What were they?

US nuclear weapon programmes

Since the election of President Reagan in 1980, the USA has been engaged in a massive modernization programme for its nuclear weapons. US forces are divided into three categories (known as the strategic Triad): land-based missiles (ICBMs), submarine-launched missiles (SLBMs) and long-range bombers—recently being armed with cruise missiles. Each leg of the strategic Triad is being modernized. The basis of this modernization has been a perception in the United States that the Soviet Union was 'winning' the arms race and was therefore threatening US security.

The MX missile
The MX 'Peacekeeper' missile, which will be able to deliver 10–12 warheads with great accuracy against military targets, is currently being tested in the USA. It is part of a huge US nuclear modernization programme. The photograph shows the fitting of re-entry vehicles onto the MX 'bus'

It's not just a matter of numbers . . .

it's also a matter of accuracy . . .

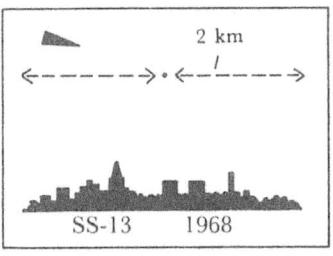

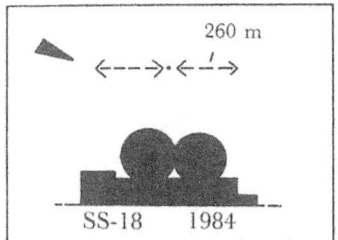

Key: Area within which half the warheads can be expected to fall. ←------→

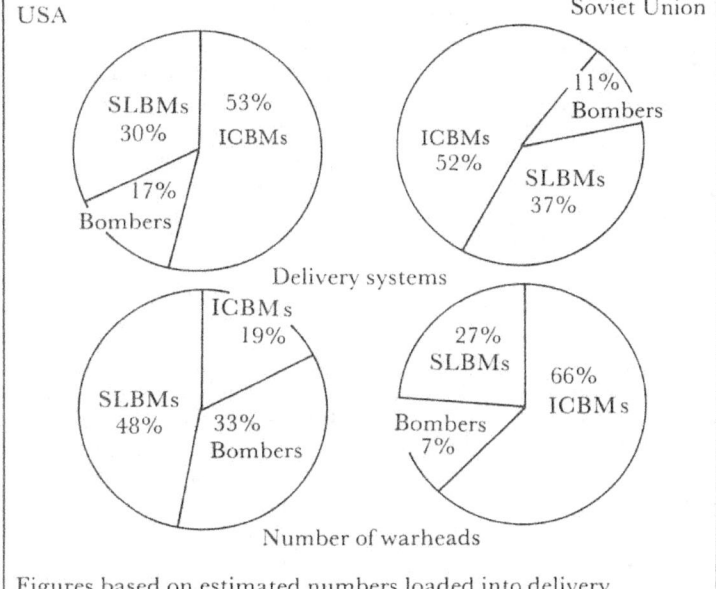

Figures based on estimated numbers loaded into delivery systems. Source: *Arkin, Arms Control Today,* June 1984; *Bulletin of the Atomic Scientists,* May 1984.

For many years politicians and negotiators have tended to compare the nuclear systems of each side in terms of numbers. But since the make-up of the Soviet and US systems are so different, different 'balances' can be produced depending on whether one chooses to compare launchers, warheads or the megatonnage of those warheads on each side.

But what really matters is what those weapons can do: it is that which is important in calculating the military balance. Therefore such factors as the increasing accuracy and decreasing flight times of nuclear systems also have to be taken into account. These factors make surprise attacks against hardened military targets easier.

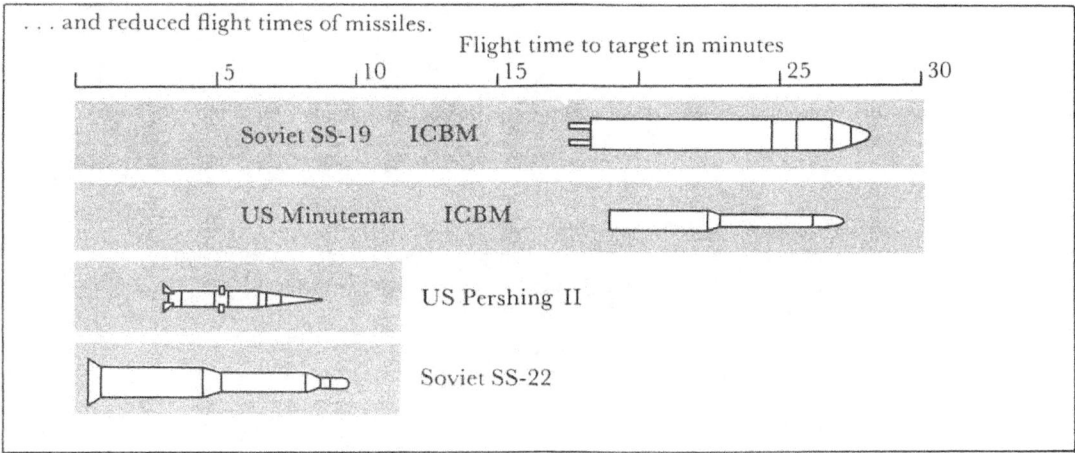

. . . and reduced flight times of missiles.

By 1984 many Americans may have felt more secure. In March President Reagan said, "I think there is less threat [to us today] ... than there was earlier when our defense was so lax that there was a window of vulnerability". But even so, there is no sign of a slow-down in the US build-up, which may imply that the goal of US nuclear policy is to regain what they perceive to be a measure of nuclear superiority over the Soviet Union. In recent years the nuclear weapon programme has consumed an increasing share of a growing defence budget, involving a sum of about $50 billion in 1984.

Strategic nuclear forces
As part of its land-based missile programme, the United States continued to develop the MX, which is a highly accurate multiple-warhead missile, of which it is planned to have 10 in place by 1987, and 100 by 1989 at a total cost of nearly $30 billion. In March 1985 the two houses of Congress approved $1.5 billion for the production of 21 MX missiles.

In 1984 a start was made on the development of a new, small single-warhead missile known as Midgetman. It is intended to produce several hundred of these, to be deployed from 1992 on mobile launchers. If the MX programme were to be cancelled, the final number of Midgetman missiles might be 1 000 or more. They will constitute a missile force, possibly mobile, with the ability to hit Soviet military targets with great accuracy.

At the end of 1984 the US nuclear submarine force consisted of 5 Trident and 31 Poseidon submarines carrying a total of 592 SLBMs. The Navy has not stated exactly how many Trident submarines it wants, though the numbers 20 and 25 are often mentioned. If 25 are eventually deployed they will be able to carry 600 Trident II missiles with a total of some 4 800 warheads at a total cost of $120 billion.

US B-1B bomber
The B-1B bomber is part of the US strategic nuclear modernization programme. It is planned to build 100. The B-1B will incorporate several elements of the latest technology such as sophisticated radars, navigational aids and jamming equipment.

US Air Force

Programmes for the strategic bomber fleet include the progressive arming of B-52s with an eventual total of 1 739 air-launched cruise missiles (ALCMs). The first 26 of an eventual total of 100 B-1B bombers are due for deployment in 1985; the rest will be deployed by 1988. This massive programme has employed thousands of workers and subcontractors throughout the USA. There may well be pressure to increase the total order beyond 100 rather than risk the economic consequences of ending the programme. These new bombers will eventually be armed with a long-range, high-speed cruise missile currently under development.

Theatre nuclear forces
During 1984 both the ground-launched cruise missile (GLCM) and the Pershing II were introduced in Europe. At the end of the year, 48 GLCMs were operational at Greenham Common in the UK, and 32 at Comiso in Italy, while 54 Pershing IIs had been deployed in West Germany. In March 1985 16 cruise missiles were deployed at Florennes in Belgium.

The nuclear-armed Tomahawk sea-launched cruise missile was first deployed in June 1984. The modernization of nuclear short-range artillery continued (possibly to be offset by the withdrawal of around 1 400 nuclear warheads from Europe) and production of a new nuclear bomb for the F-16 fighter/bomber continued. Investigations have begun into the possibility of replacing or modifying the Lance missile, and a nuclear warhead for a naval air-to-air missile is under development.

Soviet nuclear weapon programmes

The precise size of the Soviet Union's nuclear forces is open to speculation. But it is known that Soviet strategic forces are not as evenly divided as the US ones. Nearly 70 per cent of Soviet strategic warheads are deployed on land-based missiles. The Soviet Union is anxious to improve its submarine-based weapons. In the past, nearly every analysis of the US–Soviet 'balance' has credited the Soviet Union with an advantage in throw-weight (the weight the rockets can carry) and megatonnage (the total explosive yield) of nuclear missiles while the USA has been ahead in the number of warheads. This belief was brought into question when President Reagan presented new analyses which showed that the Soviet Union in fact now had a 25 per cent advantage in warheads. As with most intelligence reports, it is impossible to know how accurate such estimates are.

But there is much evidence that previous US estimates of Soviet strength have been exaggerated. And, in any case, a mere preponderance in numbers by one side over the other

ALCM
Air-launched cruise missile. A small, subsonic air-to-surface missile with a range of around 2 500 km. It carries a 200 kt nuclear warhead to within 30 m of its target. B-52 bombers are being modified to carry 12 ALCMs on external pylons and up to 8 on internal rotary launchers. The B-1B will be able to carry up to 22.

GLCM
Ground-launched cruise missile, currently being deployed in Western Europe. The missile is fired from a transporter–erector–launcher vehicle. Its range is about 2 500 km and it carries a 10–50 kt warhead. It is accurate to within a 30 m radius of its target.

does not confer any necessary advantage since both sides already possess a full range of strategic and theatre systems, more than adequate in number to cover all likely targets. It is becoming less useful to compare Soviet and US strengths in terms of numbers (even if they can be accurately determined).

New weapon technology, war-fighting strategies and perceptions of the threat posed by the enemy are more important factors in propelling the arms race. As with deterrence, the concept of strategic balance has more to do with what people think is true than with actual capabilities. Neither superpower wishes to be seen as inferior, since they believe that such an image might put them at a disadvantage in world affairs. In the words of Richard Burt, Assistant Secretary of State in the Reagan Administration, "The strategic nuclear balance is what the world understands as to who is ahead. It is a psychological as much as a hardware dimension".

Thus the concept of nuclear balance is complicated and does not make clear whether one is talking in terms of numbers of weapon systems or of the perceptions each side has of the threat posed by the other. The demand for equality or parity in nuclear weapons arises from political considerations. In military terms, sufficiency is all that is demanded for deterrence to operate; it is necessary only to possess the means, if attacked, to retaliate and inflict upon an opponent an unacceptable amount of damage. However, it is clear that neither superpower has really been prepared to accept the idea of minimum deterrence which sufficiency would imply.

Soviet secrecy has enabled estimates of Soviet superiority to be used to mobilize public support in the USA and Europe for the deployment of new weapon systems. And, in turn, rearmament in the USA and Europe has been used by the Soviet Union as the justification of its own modernization plans.

Strategic nuclear forces
The Soviet Union carried out tests on several new strategic ICBMs and rocket motors in 1984 and made preparations for new sites ready for eventual deployment. There is very little room for improvement in the Soviet land-based strategic missile force without breaching the ceilings laid down by the SALT II agreement, which both superpowers have so far kept to even though the US Congress has not endorsed it. The Soviet Union is prevented, under the terms of the treaty, from adding further new missiles and can only improve capabilities a little.

Nearly 30 per cent of the Soviet Union's strategic weapons are submarine-launched. The Soviet Union is gradually introducing more accurate SLBMs and indeed new submarines (known as the Typhoon Class) to launch them from. With increased numbers of MIRVs on these new missiles, the Soviet Union is increasing the size and power of its sea-based forces and improving the ability of its SLBMs to strike military targets (which requires considerable accuracy).

Improvements are also taking place in the Soviet Union's long-range strategic bomber force, which is being modified to carry cruise missiles including at least one new long-range type. This weapon will also be carried by the new Blackjack bomber which may first enter service during 1985.

Thus, in strategic terms, technological developments and improvements are occurring in the Soviet Union that are in many ways similar to what is happening in the United States. However, there can be little doubt that, in general, the USA has a technological lead. This is most significant in terms of submarine and bomber forces. Recent US plans for SDI, if pursued, are certain to give the USA a greater technological lead, while compelling the Soviet Union to develop countermeasures such as weapons for attacking space-based weapons and other satellites, and cruise missiles to evade the ballistic missile defences.

Theatre nuclear forces
The Soviet Union is continuing a major build-up of theatre nuclear forces involving some seven land-based missile and artillery systems. The SS-20 programme is continuing, according to NATO, with two additional bases coming into service in 1984, and nine additional bases each with nine launchers believed to be under construction. NATO figures suggest that, by the end of 1984, 396 SS-20s had been deployed. The Soviet Union denies this claim. This is an important issue because the Netherlands has said that it will

The Soviet SS-20
The SS-20 is part of the modernization programme of the Soviet Union's intermediate-range nuclear forces. It can deliver three accurate MIRVs and, as this artist's impression shows, it is carried on mobile launchers which makes it less vulnerable to attack.

US Department of Defense

only take its projected share of 48 cruise missiles if the Soviet Union has increased the number of SS-20s above 378, and will decide in November. On 7 April Mr Gorbachev announced that the Soviet Union was freezing, until November, deployment of SS-20s targeted on Europe.

But what is equally significant is that, for the first time, tactical weapons such as the SS-12 and SS-22 with ranges of over 800 km are being deployed in forward positions in both East Germany and Czechoslovakia. This is asserted to be a response to Pershing and cruise missile deployments by NATO. Other new tactical missiles are under development and new nuclear-capable howitzers are being introduced.

The Soviet Union has also continued development of its own GLCM which, with a range of about 3 000 km, is due for deployment in 1986. A larger, longer-range cruise missile which also has the ability to attack hardened military targets may be in service before the end of the decade.

The Soviet Navy has introduced some new destroyers and cruisers and has adapted some others to take cruise missiles. US satellite photographs have shown a nuclear-powered aircraft-carrier currently under construction. Some accidents befell Soviet weapon systems in 1984: a cruise missile, when being tested, flew off in the wrong direction across Norwegian airspace before crashing in Finland; and two submarine collisions were also reported.

The nuclear weapon programmes of other countries

Present modernization plans for nuclear forces in both the UK and France involve substantial MIRVing programmes, which will bring their warhead totals to about 2 000 in the 1990s. At this figure, the nuclear forces of France and Britain can no longer be regarded as negligible, and there will be understandable pressure from the Soviet Union, which has hitherto been resisted, to count French and British nuclear forces in any arms control agreement covering offensive nuclear weapons.

The *United Kingdom* has continued to replace the warheads on its submarine-launched missiles with the new Chevaline warhead. Major orders were placed in 1984 for its Trident missile, which will replace the existing Polaris fleet in the 1990s, and will increase the number of nuclear warheads very substantially.

The British front-line defence forces in Europe have been further strengthened by the positioning in forward bases in West Germany of the Tornado strike aircraft (which is nuclear-capable). The Tornado programme will result in an increase in the number of nuclear-capable aircraft stationed in West Germany. This will probably increase Britain's stockpile of nuclear bombs, particularly as some of the

Panavia Aircraft GmbH

Jaguar and Buccaneer aircraft withdrawn from West Germany may retain a nuclear strike role when stationed in the United Kingdom.

France is about to introduce into service a new MIRVed SLBM. Furthermore, in July 1984 the new Mirage 2000 fighter was first deployed. One version of it is designed for a nuclear attack role. Development work continues on France's first nuclear-armed air-to-surface missile which will have both strategic and tactical roles, being carried both on the Mirage and the Super Etendard fighters.

In *China* the nuclear missile programme has received priority within a generally restricted budget. New submarine-launched missiles are under development, and three submarines are reported to be under construction.

Nuclear sea-launched cruise missiles

The USA is introducing modern SLCMs into its navy. By doing this it is extending the range and role of naval firepower, which is likely to play a part in a wide range of nuclear war-fighting plans. For the US Navy, the SLCM offers the opportunity to strike specific sea and land targets with great accuracy from a great distance. Targets deep within enemy territory, including hardened military targets, that have been beyond range up till now, can be hit with a high probability of success. At present, the USA has a lead over the Soviet Union in this kind of technology. There can be little doubt that the Soviet Union is developing matching systems which will eventually be deployed to counter US capabilities.

The multi-role Tornado
The Panavia Tornado IDS (interdiction/strike) version can carry both nuclear and conventional weapons over a combat radius of 1 400 km. It is a joint British, German and Italian product. More than 500 aircraft will be acquired for theatre missions. Others are deployed for naval support and (in another variant) for air defence roles.

For the USA, the Tomahawk cruise missile is a cheap and effective way of increasing substantially the number of ships from which long-range nuclear strikes can be made. This has until recently been confined to the USA's 14 aircraft-carriers; but the SLCM will allow that figure to increase to 200 ships and submarines (in addition to the plans for SSBNs). 3 994 Tomahawk cruise missiles are planned for production; of these, 2 739 will be for surface ships, and the rest for submarines. Preparing these ships will not be very expensive because the cruise missiles can be fired from existing torpedo tubes or from vertical launchers which are easy to install.

Taken together, these two factors represent a very considerable increase in the ability of the USA to project itself militarily in areas of the world far away from home. This must worry the Soviet Union a great deal, especially since, as the US Navy asserted in 1984, the Tomahawk's presence around the borders of the Soviet Union will "convey to the Soviet Union that its territory is not a sanctuary".

It is impossible for an adversary to tell whether a cruise missile carries a nuclear or a conventional warhead until it reaches its target. This factor and the deployment of the SLCM (and indeed the cruise missile in general) in large numbers has raised very difficult problems for any future negotiations on arms control measures.

SSBN
Ballistic missile-equipped, nuclear-powered submarine.

SLCM
The deployment of the sea-launched Tomahawk cruise missile represents a very large increase in the capabilities of the US Navy. The SLCM can carry either a conventional or a nuclear warhead over distances of up to 2 500 km. It can be fired from submarines and from the decks of specially converted surface ships. This series of pictures shows a test launch from the destroyer USS Merrill in March 1983.

US Department of Defense

Space weapons

Space has become the new frontier of the arms race. The superpowers are poised to take their arms competition into this new arena by placing weapons in space. If they do so, the consequences may be awesome. Both superpowers already possess limited capabilities for attacking some satellites. These are known as anti-satellite (ASAT) weapons. But what is currently proposed by the USA is a system of defence against ballistic missiles which would make extensive use of space weapons. This is known officially as the Strategic Defense Initiative (SDI), but most people know it by its popular description: Star Wars. The Soviet Union has also been improving its existing anti-ballistic missile defences and may have plans for extending them. As research moves on to the testing stage of possible space defences, there will be serious consequences both for existing international arms control agreements and for the prospects of future arms control negotiations between the superpowers. This chapter will consider these issues.

ASAT
Anti-satellite. ASAT weapons are a part of a system for destroying, damaging or disturbing the normal working of, or changing the flight path of, artificial earth satellites.

US NAVSTAR satellite
Satellites perform important military roles in communications and navigation. With the help of navigation satellites such as the US NAVSTAR pictured here, it is possible to guide nuclear warheads to their targets with very great accuracy.

US Air Force

ASAT weapons

Satellites are the eyes and ears of the military. About 75 per cent of the 2 200 or more satellites so far launched have some military application. There are several different uses for military satellites. Large numbers of satellites are used for reconnaissance—many have been launched to take pictures of enemy positions and forces while others monitor the opponent's radio signals. Communications satellites relay messages between commanders and their forces. A third group allows military unit and submarine commanders to identify their positions with pin-point accuracy. These three functions are the most important, although military satellites are also involved in mapping and monitoring weather conditions.

The central importance of satellites to the superpowers is illustrated by their role in nuclear war-fighting. Satellites would give the first warning of the launch of enemy missiles. They would be vital channels through which commanders could instruct their units as to what retaliatory action to take, and for assessing the development of the battle. Satellites are also needed for guiding bombers, submarines and missiles on the way to their targets. They also update the precise targeting instructions programmed into the navigational instruments on missiles fired from moving platforms such as submarines. Furthermore, if current SDI proposals lead to eventual testing and deployment stages, satellites would also be employed in identifying and tracking incoming missiles in order to guide anti-ballistic missile (ABM) warheads onto their targets.

It is therefore hardly surprising that satellites make tempting targets. Because of their central role in battle management, it is widely believed that they would be priority targets at the beginning of hostilities. Up till recently the means available for attacking satellites have been quite crude and the superpowers have put many more resources into the development of other areas. Since at least 1963, the Soviet Union has been developing an ASAT system to damage enemy satellites. It uses a 'killer' satellite which, after being lobbed into orbit by rocket, creeps up on the target satellite and destroys it on receiving instructions from the ground. It is a rather cumbersome and slow system which can only threaten satellites that are in low orbit. Although the Soviet system is still considered to be operational, it does not appear to have been tested since 1982.

The USA had an operating ASAT system which was deployed from 1964 until 1975. It relied on using a Thor missile to throw a nuclear warhead at a satellite. When it turned out that it would probably do as much damage to

The Soviet ASAT system

1 Cosmos interceptor in elliptical orbit

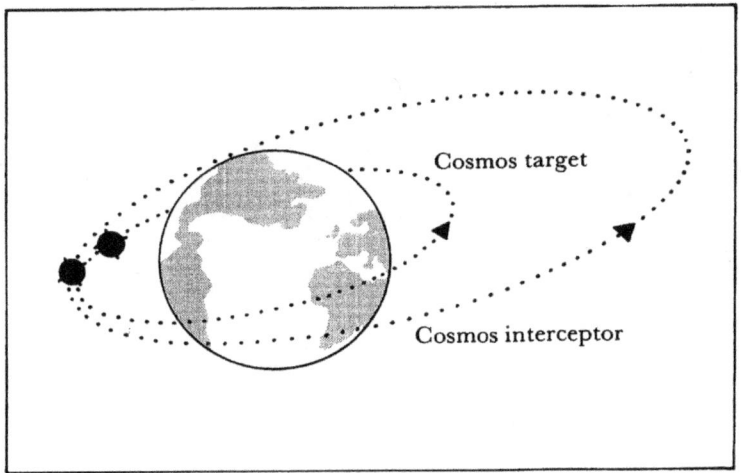

2 Cosmos intentionally destroyed

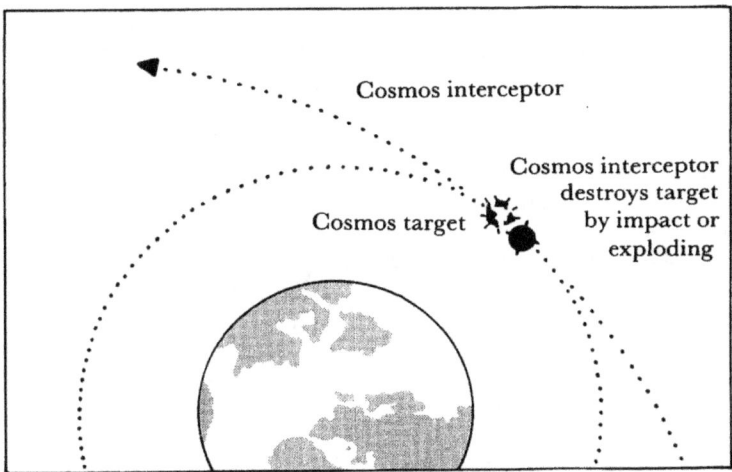

US spacecraft as to Soviet ones, the programme was discontinued. However, in the mid- to late-1970s US interest in ASAT was rekindled. The system now being tested relies on a heat-seeking missile launched from an F-15 fighter. The 'warhead' does not explode. It does its damage simply by colliding with the satellite, which is enough to put it out of action. The new US ASAT programme has greater potential than the Soviet one. It is fast: the missile can be on its way in a matter of minutes, whereas the Soviet one takes many hours. Furthermore, it can be launched from anywhere in the world where F-15s can take off. The Soviet system has to wait for satellites to

US Department of Defense

F-15 carrying ASAT weapon
Both superpowers have been developing ASAT systems for the destruction of low-orbit satellites. The Soviet system relies on hunter-killer satellites, while the US development uses an infra-red guided missile which can be launched from an F-15 fighter.

come into the correct zone for attack, or the weapon has to make several orbital manoeuvres in order to intercept the target. However, like the Soviet ASAT system, it can also only engage satellites in low orbit.

If ASAT technology is further developed there will be considerable risk of destabilization. If, for example, a satellite stopped working, the other side's ASAT would be the first suspect. If indeed it was believed that one's satellite had been attacked this could be regarded as an act of war. If one side were able to knock out the other's satellites before they could be used to co-ordinate an attack, this would be a tremendous advantage in a global conflict. There would therefore be a considerable temptation to launch such a pre-emptive strike.

The Soviet Union in 1983 proposed a treaty that would ban the testing or deployment of weapons in space. The proposal covered both weapons trained on the Earth from space and any weapons (wherever based) aimed at spacecraft. The USA has rejected the Soviet proposals on the grounds that such a ban would be hard to verify. Too many different weapons could be used to attack satellites. The launchers employed have many other purposes so that it would be hard to ban their use as anti-satellite weapons while permitting their use for other purposes.

The Soviet proposals might also arguably inhibit the development of a system of ballistic missile defence such as the one currently being researched in the USA. What are the implications of this research programme?

Star Wars

The US proposal for a comprehensive defence screen to protect the United States and its allies from ballistic missile attack has been presented as the single most radical development in the nuclear field in recent years. Because the system is largely based on space weapons and would utilize some exotic technology, it has been dubbed as Star Wars. Among popular candidates for this ambitious task are lasers and kinetic energy weapons such as electro-magnetic railguns.

The implications of SDI are massive. First, it will be a very expensive programme indeed, especially since it is on a grand scale and because much of the technology it would employ is at an early stage of development. Its appeal to the general public is based on its presentation as an impenetrable shield behind which the population could remain, secure in the knowledge that, as President Reagan put it, SDI would have rendered nuclear weapons "obsolete". It also appeals in this form because it is presented as a defence system which dispenses with "dirty" nuclear weapons.

It also counters moral arguments which can be made against Mutual Assured Destruction (MAD) because it seems to offer the possibility of the USA moving away from a nuclear strategy which threatens to kill millions of innocent people if deterrence fails to one which simply provides security for the country that might be the victim of attack. The argument is complete when it is suggested that such security would render a nuclear attack pointless. Thus, Star Wars has been presented as a non-threatening defence, as the ultimate defender of peace. As President Reagan said in February 1985, "The only program we have [at present] is MAD—Mutual Assured Destruction. Why don't we have MAS instead—Mutual Assured Security?".

SDI is conceived as a layered defence system. More accurately, it is a number of systems linked together. The first layer of the system would attempt to knock out enemy missiles soon after launch, in the few minutes of their boost phase, as they climbed through the Earth's atmosphere. The second layer or system attacks the warheads or re-entry vehicles as well as the small 'bus' which aims and dispenses the MIRVs. A third layer would intercept warheads in mid-course. This space-based system would have 20–25 minutes to deal with the thousands of warheads involved in an intercontinental mass attack. Any surviving warheads would then be intercepted, during the last minute or two before reaching their targets, by a terminal defence system based on Earth. This might involve quick-reaction non-nuclear missiles which would launch homing interceptors on the incoming warheads while still above the atmosphere. The USA successfully tested such an interception in 1984.

SDI did not emerge overnight. The USA—and, for that matter, the Soviet Union too—has been developing and testing various elements of a potential ballistic missile defence programme since the early 1970s. One successful test does not necessarily mean that SDI, as presented to the general public, is feasible. To create a perfect defence system it would need to intercept some 8 000 warheads aimed at widely dispersed targets across the USA, and to do so within half an hour of first warning. Its critics argue that SDI just will not work. There is no system, they argue, that could ever be devised which could guarantee 100 per cent success against an incoming missile attack. Nor, they say,

Star Wars: layered defence against ballistic missile attack
The diagram shows how a layered defence system against ballistic missile attack might work. For simplicity, the diagram only shows single missiles. In reality there might be thousands involved. Similarly, there would be many more SDI platforms. The four layers of the defence might be as follows. An early-warning satellite (1) picks up the rocket launch. The first layer is a laser (2) which attacks rockets as they are climbing out of the earth's atmosphere. In the second layer, the 'bus' which dispenses the warheads and decoys is attacked by an electro-magnetic railgun (3). In the mid-course phase of the defence, a target-acquisition and tracking satellite (4) locates and passes on information about the surviving warheads so that they can be attacked by, for example, another laser (5). The fourth layer is the terminal defence. In this, an infra-red probe (6) is sent into space to relay information about the trajectories of the remaining incoming warheads and to discriminate between live warheads and decoys. The warheads are intercepted by non-nuclear devices (7) which, after launch by rocket, home in using infra-red heat-seeking sensors.

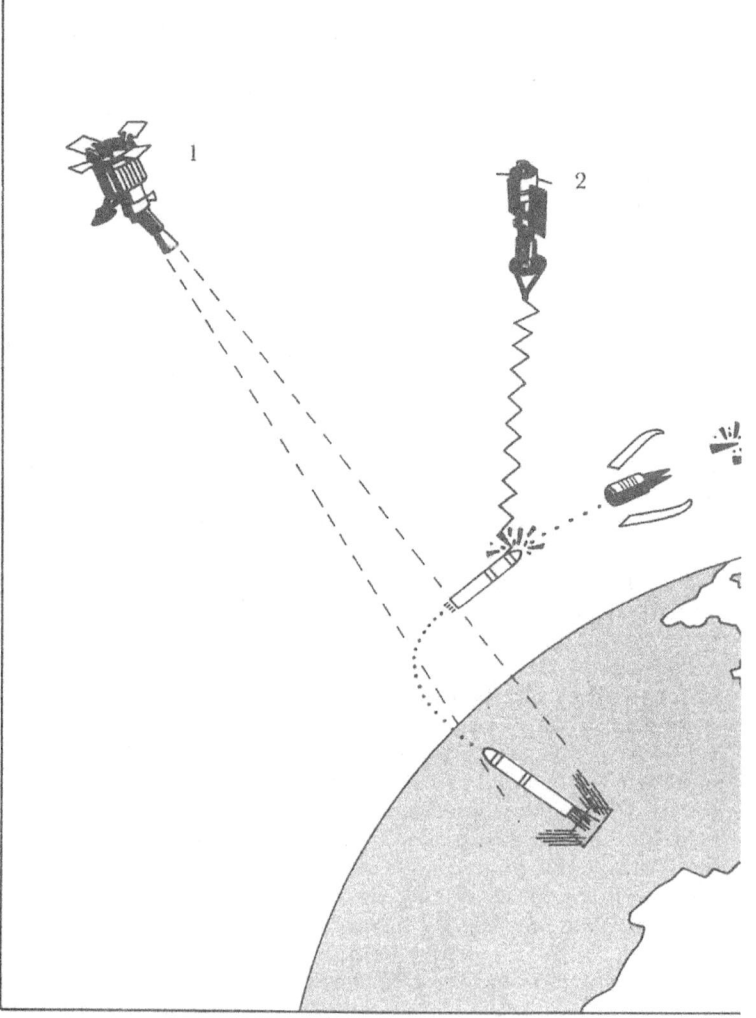

could it handle cruise missiles, bombers and submarines deployed close to US coastlines. Even assuming it worked first time and assuming further that it had a remarkable 99.9 per cent success rate, that would still allow through 8 warheads in an 8 000-warhead attack. If they fell on cities it could mean millions of deaths. The impenetrable screen has, the critics say, that other feature of Star Wars—fantasy.

It is perhaps more realistic to see SDI as a system to defend missile silos from attack, which is, indeed, the aspect the USA now stresses. By defending ICBM silos it could limit the damage of an attack so that the ICBM forces would be able to retaliate. 100 per cent success does not, in this case, have to be achieved.

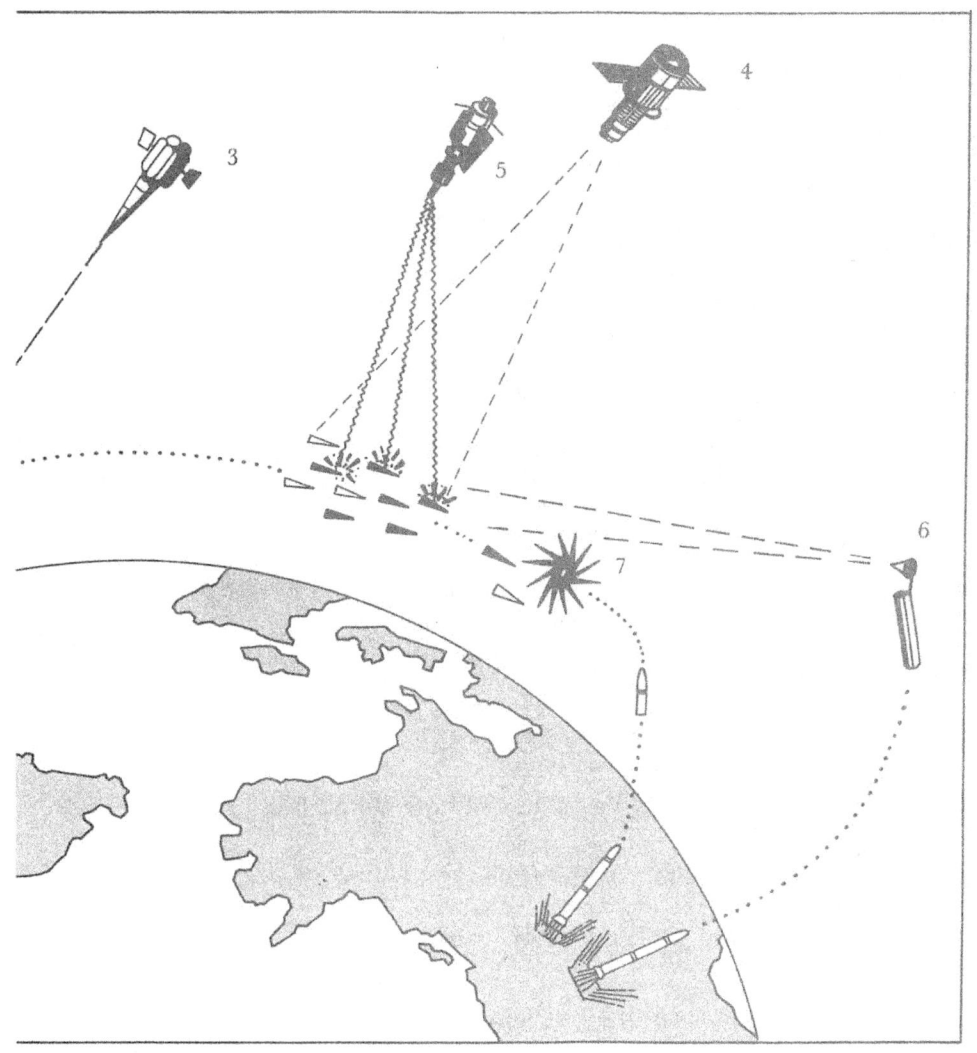

The supporters of SDI argue that, although the defence of cities may be impossible at present, this does not make it impossible for all time. Further, they claim that SDI will increase the stability of the relations between the superpowers because, by increasing reliance on defensive systems, it will become easier to negotiate a reduction in offensive weapons. They contend that it is not sensible for the USA to continue to base its defence strategy entirely upon the concept of MAD. The increasing accuracy of offensive missiles will, they say, render nuclear forces increasingly vulnerable to pre-emptive attack. If effective retaliation cannot be guaranteed, deterrence is undermined. Thus, in the long run, SDI would offer a better chance of maintaining world peace than the continued threat of mutual annihilation.

Against this view it can be argued that SDI is futile. Its critics suggest that it could never be successful because the Soviet Union could easily develop countermeasures to undermine it. It is also suggested that SDI will be destabilizing because it will trigger off yet another lap in the arms race. Far from encouraging the Soviet Union to reduce its reliance upon offensive weapons in favour of a defensive shield similar in function to the SDI, it may well have the opposite effect. The Soviet Union may decide to build up the level of its offensive arsenal as a countermeasure to SDI. It could overwhelm any particular level of SDI simply by increasing the number of missiles and warheads aimed against the USA. SDI is specifically aimed at defending against ballistic missiles. The Soviet Union could therefore make greater use of cruise missiles which could evade the defences. Moreover the Soviet Union, it is suggested, could build and deploy these countermeasures at a fraction of the cost of the ABM systems themselves.

The SDI plans are also criticized for being destabilizing in another respect. The Soviet Union claims that SDI is not a purely defensive system but a shield to accompany a first strike, for it could be an effective barrier against weakened Soviet retaliatory forces. If this is a genuine fear on the part of the Soviet Union, it could, in a crisis, be tempted to launch a pre-emptive strike against the defensive space stations and other satellites.

SDI and ASAT systems are closely enmeshed. SDI envisages the use of space-based sensors for the tracking of enemy missiles. But these sensors would be vulnerable to ASAT weapons. At the same time, the technology required to set up an effective defence against ballistic missiles would also facilitate the deployment of an extremely effective ASAT system. Satellites are much easier targets than missiles. Indeed, the platforms on which SDI weapons would be mounted in space would have a dual function: the destruction of the enemy's satellites and the interception and destruction of incoming warheads.

Ironically, then, SDI contributes to ASAT development but improvements in ASAT undermine SDI. If the USA goes ahead with SDI it will boost the development of long-range ASAT weapons—not only would this threaten the satellite-tracking and reconnaissance systems of the Soviet Union but it could also put the safety of early-warning satellites in doubt. In this sense, SDI development efforts would be very destabilizing even if they never produced a workable ballistic missile defence system.

The implications for arms control

Except for one system of limited radius, protecting one defined area, both the Soviet Union and the USA are prevented, by the ABM Treaty of 1972, from developing, testing or deploying "ABM systems which are sea-based, air-based, space-based or mobile land-based". Depending upon one's interpretation of the treaty as a whole, this would arguably rule out the SDI programme because it largely relies on space-based systems. The USA must either

Warhead used in homing overlay experiment
This is a non-explosive 'warhead' like the one which successfully intercepted an incoming ICBM re-entry vehicle in June 1984. Launched by rocket, a 'homing-and-kill' vehicle puts the device on a collision course with the target re-entry vehicle using an infra-red sensor to locate it. The metal ribs of the 'warhead' (over 2 m long and studded with metal weights) unfurl seconds before impact and collide with the target.

US Department of Defense

soon give up the development of space-based defence or abrogate the treaty.

The treaty does have a clause which would allow either party to withdraw if it decides that "extraordinary events related to the subject matter of the treaty have jeopardised its supreme interests". Recently the USA has criticized the Soviet Union for breaking the terms of the treaty by developing a large radar system which, they allege, would allow the Soviet Union to have an ABM capability much broader than the restricted area allowed by the treaty. The USA has not so far suggested that the existence of the radar system is grounds for its withdrawal from the treaty. On the other hand, some people argue that the testing of the non-explosive warhead for the terminal phase of SDI was a breach of the ABM Treaty, because it was launched by a Minuteman missile which is not an ABM launcher permitted by the treaty.

Apart from the SALT II agreement of 1979 (which has never been ratified by the USA), the ABM Treaty is the only significant arms control measure to have been agreed between the superpowers for 14 years. It is now under threat. The Soviet Union has no good reason for wanting to see it go since its ABM technology is considerably inferior to that of the USA. But, although research into ABM systems is not forbidden by the treaty, the US plans for ballistic missile defence clearly are incompatible with the spirit of it. Whether the USA will choose to abrogate it, or try to renegotiate it perhaps in combination with proposals to radically reduce the number of offensive missiles on both sides, and to share some of the ABM technology with the Soviet Union (as some US politicians have suggested) remains to be seen. But the option of dropping the Star Wars venture is not a possibility that the present Administration seems prepared to contemplate.

Chemical and biological warfare

Chemical armaments

Until recently there appears to have been a period of quiescence as far as chemical weapons are concerned. This period seems to be coming to an end. For 15 years from 1969 the USA has made no filled chemical munitions, but recently there has been growing pressure within NATO for chemical rearmament.

The Geneva Protocol of 1925 prohibits the use of chemical and biological weapons, but it does not ban the development of such weapons; and several of the countries that signed the Protocol (including the USA and the Soviet Union) have argued that, while they will abide by the terms of the treaty, they nevertheless reserve the right to use chemical weapons in retaliation against an attack in which chemical weapons are employed. This is the justification for holding stocks of chemical weapons in those countries that have them.

The Biological Weapons Convention of 1972 goes further than the Geneva Protocol. It bans not just the use, but also the production of biological weapons. As in other areas of warfare, so long as research programmes continue, there will continually be pressure to develop new weapons. Within the USA there is a programme to develop binary nerve-gas munitions. Binaries are safer to store and handle because the various constituents of the final toxic chemical are stored separately in the binary munition and are only combined into their lethal mixture after the munition has been fired.

A number of senior officers within NATO have argued that it is necessary for NATO to have a modern chemical capability to match the threat posed by Warsaw Pact capabilities. It was further suggested that a binary nerve-gas programme would help to put pressure upon the Soviet Union to reach an acceptable chemical weapon agreement at the Conference on Disarmament in Geneva.

Additional allegations of Soviet use of chemical weapons in Afghanistan were made by the USA in 1984, basing their claims on the evidence supplied by Soviet defectors whom they described as "highly credible human sources". It is difficult to know how much reliance can be placed on such evidence.

However, there can be no doubt at all that chemical weapons were used by Iraq in the Gulf War. There are numerous documented cases of chemical attack, verified by a United Nations investigating team. Indeed, several of the most seriously injured Iranian victims were flown for treatment in Western hospitals in a full blaze of publicity. Iraq is in clear breach of the Geneva Protocol. Yet it has received no condemnation from the United Nations.

If it becomes clear that a country can resort to the use of chemical weapons with impunity then other countries will be tempted to act likewise. Unlike nuclear weapons and advanced conventional weapons, the technology for making and delivering toxic chemicals is relatively straightforward and cheap. It may be that we are on the edge of a chemical arms race. If that happens, such weapons could spread rapidly across the world. Thus the international community has very good reasons for upholding an international agreement designed to prevent this from happening.

Chemical weapons in NATO

In spite of the considerable efforts made by the Reagan Administration to persuade them, the US Congress refused, in 1984, for the third year running, to provide funds required to move from research and development to full-scale production of new binary nerve-gas weapons.

One of the weaknesses of the US Administration's arguments for the binary programme was its failure to obtain from European governments an undertaking to store additional US chemical weapons on their territory. Accordingly, from midsummer onwards there appears to have been a concerted effort to mould European opinion to accept this idea. Various high-ranking military officers, including the NATO supreme commander, General Rogers, were quoted as saying that European NATO countries required a chemical weapon retaliatory capability. General Rogers also pointed out that there were no formal procedures, such as existed with nuclear weapons, for consulting NATO governments about the use of chemical weapons.

This effort to place chemical weapons on the political agenda in Europe received cool responses from spokesmen for both the British and West German governments, denying that there was any immediate need for NATO chemical weapon armament. However, newspaper reports were to appear later in the year suggesting that, since the spring, there had been a top-level governmental review of Britain's chemical weapon policy.

The political developments in this area in 1985 will depend partly on possible shifts in government attitudes in

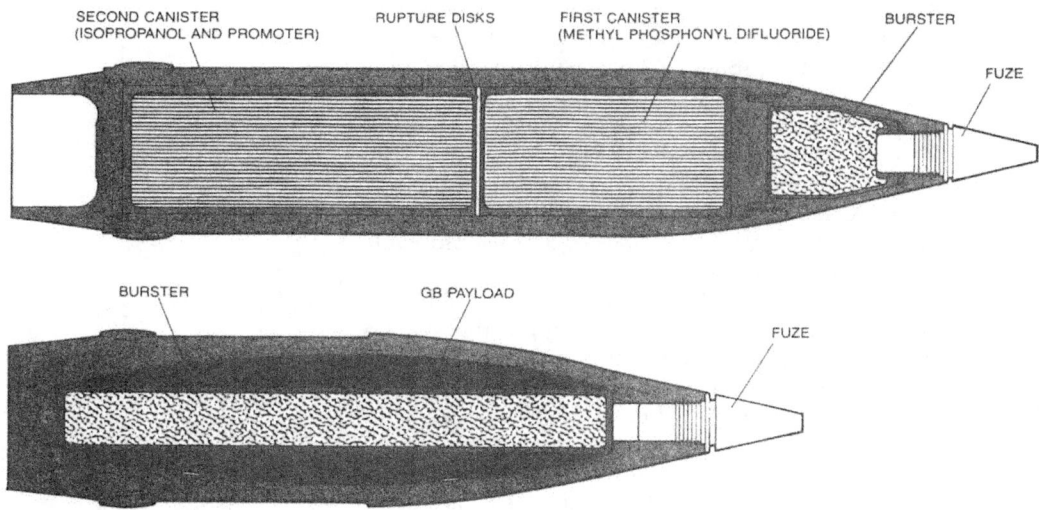

Binary nerve-gas munition
The diagram shows two 155 mm artillery shells carrying the nerve gas GB. The upper one is the new binary munition. The shell is relatively safe to store and handle because the nerve gas is only produced when the contents of the two canisters are mixed during flight. The lower shell is the non-binary equivalent which is at present stockpiled by the USA.

Britain and West Germany, and also on the Reagan Administration's success in overcoming congressional hostility to the binary programme. Congress has agreed to the setting-up of a Chemical Warfare Review Commission to look at the whole issue of chemical weapons from a non-partisan viewpoint.

Meanwhile the research and development programme continues, with designs for different ways of delivering binary munitions being undertaken. A wide range of methods is being researched. Possibilities include the options of using cruise missiles, multiple rocket launchers, land mines, 155-mm howitzer shells, and even Pershing II missiles.

In France, the only NATO country other than the USA to possess a significant chemical weapon capability (estimated to be about 435 tons of chemical weapon agent), there were signs of renewed interest in chemical weapon rearmament. The director of the French chemical weapon research and development programme concluded a report on the subject with words which he attributed to Stalin: "In a scientific war, he who prepares only for the defensive digs his own grave".

The Soviet Union and other Warsaw Pact countries

As usual, comment on the Soviet chemical weapon programme has come from Western sources. The US Army Chemical Corps repeated its assertion that "Soviet doctrine clearly states that chemical weapons will be used whenever it is advantageous". J. Hubner, a US defence analyst who has written extensively on chemical weapons, argued that a Soviet high-speed attack could work if chemical weapons were used because they could rapidly and effectively overcome NATO defences without overstraining Warsaw Pact resources. Airfields, ports, supply depots, NATO nuclear missiles, ground forces, forward defences and even cities would be probable targets.

According to the US Joint Chiefs of Staff, the imbalance of chemical weapon forces between NATO and the Warsaw Pact is being worsened by a continuing Soviet build-up. A summary of US intelligence estimates of this imbalance are listed in the reference section at the end of this book. Many reports appeared in Western publications about new Soviet delivery systems for chemical weapons including cluster bombs, battlefield missiles and ballistic missiles with 'tumbling' warheads.

It is hard to know how reliable Western estimates of Soviet chemical weapon capabilities are. Intelligence analysts claim that their information is gleaned from highly reliable sources; but Fred Kaplan, a former CIA agent who

US Department of Defense

Soviet chemical corps
The Soviet Union has a large number of soldiers specially trained in chemical warfare, and the Soviet Union has a large stockpile of chemical munitions. Anxiety about improved Soviet chemical weapon capabilities lies behind President Reagan's requests to Congress to fund the production of new chemical munitions.

was involved in a comprehensive US study of Soviet chemical weapon capabilities, said, "We really don't know a thing about how many weapons they have .... Anyone who says otherwise is kidding himself".

Chemical warfare in 1984

It was argued by several writers in 1984 that the chemical weapon programmes of the superpowers would provide strong incentives for other countries to produce their own chemical weapon armouries.

As mentioned earlier, the most clear and undisputed evidence of the use of chemical weapons has come from the war between Iran and Iraq. The Iranian authorities have alleged that Iraq has used chemical weapons on more than 130 occasions since 1980, but mostly in 1984. In these, at least 3 500 people have been killed or injured. The Iranians allowed outside observers to visit alleged chemical weapon victims being treated in Iran. In addition, about 70 seriously injured patients were flown to nine countries for intensive treatment. By the end of March a team of UN investigators was able to prove beyond reasonable doubt that mustard gas had been used against Iranian soldiers.

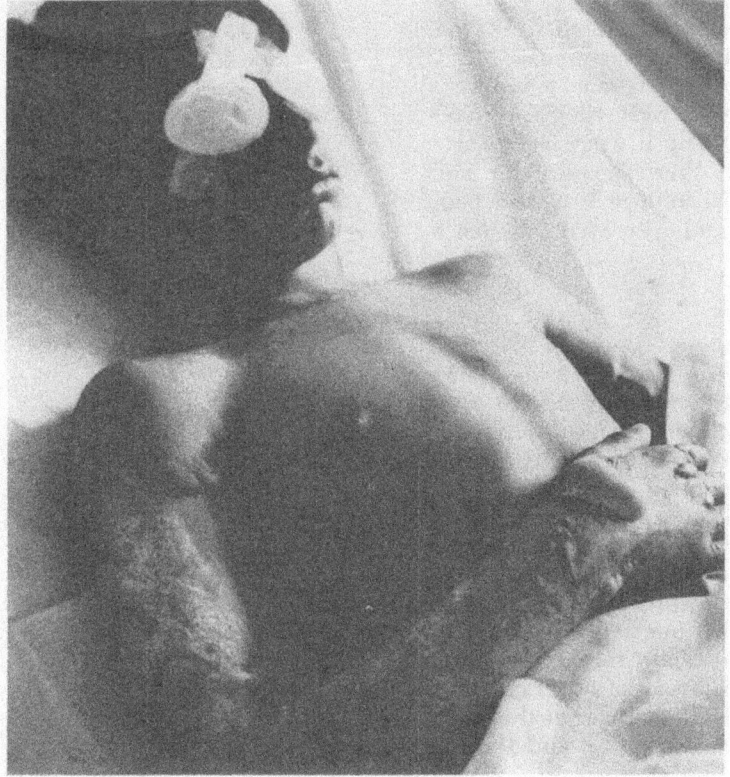

Iranian victim of Iraqi chemical attack
An Iranian victim of a chemical attack, possibly with mustard gas, during fighting in the Gulf War in 1984.

Despite this proof the UN was unable formally to condemn Iraq for breaking the 1925 Geneva Protocol, owing to opposition from, among others, the Soviet Union. The Secretary-General did call upon both warring parties to declare that they would not resort to chemical weapons. Iran did so; Iraq did not. While condemning the use of chemical weapons in general, neither the UN Security Council nor the UN General Assembly mentioned Iraq by name.

The Iraqi use of chemical weapons clearly raises the possibility that there may be more countries possessing such weapons than had previously been supposed. Before 1984 only the USA, the Soviet Union and France were confirmed possessors of chemical weapons, although allegations of secret production had been made against another 20 countries during the previous decade. By the end of 1984, that estimate had risen to 30 countries. Countries mentioned in a report from the US Defense Department included Egypt, Iraq, Viet Nam and North Korea. Press articles, quoting CIA reports, listed such countries as Libya, Israel, Ethiopia, Burma, China, Cuba and Peru. SWAPO (the Namibian Liberation movement) and the PLO were mentioned as recipients of chemical weapons.

The Soviet Union denied any involvement in spreading chemical weapons to other countries, but accused the CIA of issuing chemical weapons to the Afghan "counter-revolutionaries". Several countries were alleged to have supplied Iraq with materials to help it wage chemical warfare. By the summer, many Western countries had placed embargoes on the export, both to Iraq and Iran, of chemicals and equipment that could be used for such a purpose.

Biological weapons

The Biological Weapons Convention of 1972 bans the development, possession and use of biological and toxin weapons. Several official publications in the USA have accused the Soviet Union of breaking the treaty by having established a number of centres to study the usefulness of biological weapons and several other installations to produce and store such weapons. A US Defense Department report cited further evidence that a biological weapon research establishment in Sverdlovsk accidently released anthrax spores into the air in 1979 which infected the local population. The Soviet authorities attributed the epidemic to meat tainted by a natural outbreak of anthrax.

The Soviet Union also repeated claims that the USA had used biological weapons in Cuba, Pakistan and India in the previous 13 years.

As we have seen repeatedly so far, most of the information concerning chemical and biological weapons comes from intelligence sources, and as such is very difficult to check. As one particular case clearly illustrates, the reliability of such intelligence work is open to question.

The issue of Yellow Rain emerged in 1983. The US government announced that it had evidence that Vietnamese forces were using Soviet-supplied toxic substances derived from a highly poisonous mould fungus. This came to be known as Yellow Rain, as refugees and villagers who were interviewed about it described the yellow poison as falling from the sky. Several samples were collected for laboratory investigation in order to provide hard evidence for the public accusations which the US government was making.

One of the discoveries was that all the samples tested for pollen were found to contain pollen. The US State Department therefore accused the Soviet Union of using pollen to propagate biological weapons. However, on analysis, the pollen was traced to a wide range of different South-East Asian plants. It seemed unlikely that the Soviet Union would make the effort to collect different samples of pollen for their war effort. Towards the end of 1984 laboratory studies seemed to be showing that most, if not all, of the samples collected were in fact bee droppings. Where the samples did contain toxins (and only some did) it is possible that they arose from normal environmental factors. There are documented examples of "mass defecation" by swarms of bees. And it appears increasingly likely that that is what Yellow Rain is.

Reflecting the failure to find hard evidence to support the Yellow Rain argument (including the failure to find any spent rounds of toxic-agent ammunition after eight years of alleged use in South-East Asia), the tone of argument from US defence sources became less confident. In March 1984 an Assistant Defense Secretary was quoted as saying that the evidence was "very good" and that the Administration had "high confidence in it". In July, when asked about the bee-dropping explanation for Yellow Rain, the director of the US Arms Control and Disarmament Agency agreed that there was indeed "confusion on that issue". Despite this, however, US officials are continuing to make the allegation.

Interest is now beginning to wane in this alleged chemical and biological weapon treaty violation. Because it is still unresolved, it tends to create an unjustified belief in widespread breaking of chemical and biological weapon treaties. Such a belief is both an obstacle to arms control negotiations and may, as suggested earlier, act as an incentive to other countries to develop a chemical and biological weapon capability.

Major events during 1984

Evidence is still emerging about the widespread and horrific effects of the use of Agent Orange by US forces in Indo-China in the 1960s. There are still numerous outstanding claims in the USA by former servicemen who believe that they and their offspring have been damaged by the chemical. In Brazil, where a similar chemical has been used in clearing large tracts of the Amazon rain forest, there have been reports of mass poisonings and birth deformities linked to the chemical.

Bhopal

The most significant chemical accident of 1984 must be the tragic release on 3 December of methyl isocyanate over large parts of the Indian city of Bhopal. At least 2 500 people were killed and probably 50 times that number injured. The chemical which did this damage was held in underground bulk storage tanks for the manufacture of pesticides. The accident indicates that there is a need to negotiate a tighter control over chemical production as part of a wider agreement on the control of chemical weapons. Modern nerve gases are up to 100 times more deadly than the chemical involved at Bhopal.

World military expenditure and arms production

In recent years world expenditure on the military sector has been accelerating, from an average of 2.4 per cent a year in the late 1970s to 3.6 per cent in the 1980s. Expenditure on military research and development has accelerated even faster, from something under 1 per cent growth per year in the late 1970s to between 6 and 9 per cent in the 1980s.

In 1984 world military spending reached a total of around $800 billion. The main impetus behind these figures is the massive rearmament programme of the USA, where military spending has been rising very fast indeed—by 9.2 per cent a year since 1981. While military expenditure figures say little about the relative military strength of countries, they do give us an indication of the level of international and domestic tension and of the amount of money that could have been used for other investment purposes and to develop social and welfare programmes if the money had not gone into armaments instead.

Constant prices
Because price inflation occurs in most economies, tables of figures which compare spending from one year to another would be distorted if changes due to inflation were not eliminated. It would not be possible to tell whether, for example, spending had risen because of inflation or for other reasons. In this book we use constant prices when comparing figures for different years. If a date is given, that is the year which is taken as the base line for comparisons.

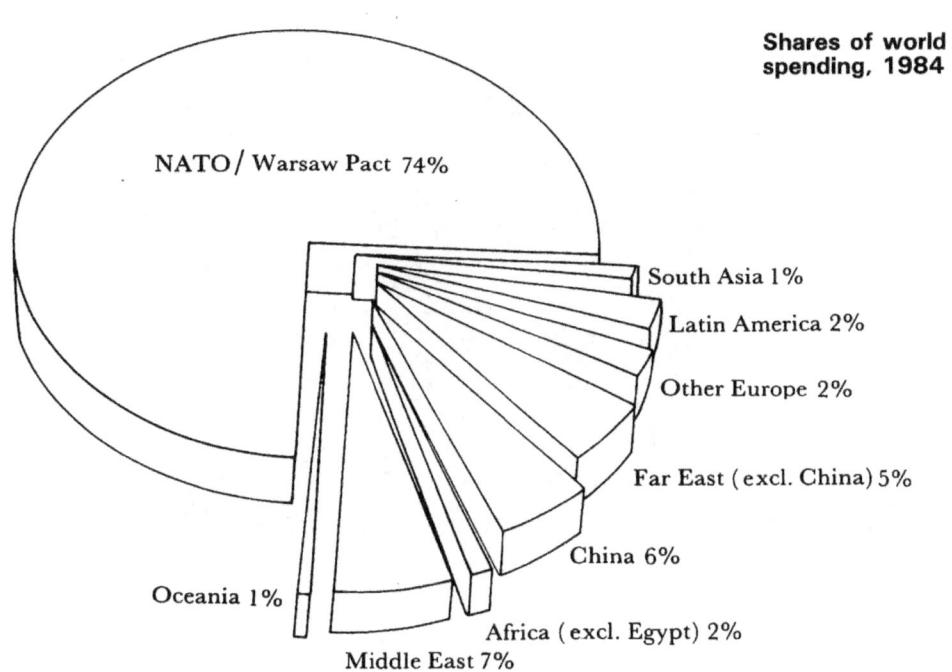

Shares of world military spending, 1984

The USA

The massive rearmament programme undertaken by the present US Administration over the past four years has resulted in a level of military spending about 40 per cent higher than it was in 1980. If the Administration continues to have its way, spending will rise by another 40 per cent over the next five years. This huge spending spree by the USA was propelled by a public perception towards the end of the 1970s that the USA had become weaker than the Soviet Union. This inferiority complex was confirmed by the protracted crisis of the US hostages in Iran, which seemed to demonstrate that the USA could be kicked around and humiliated with impunity. It was therefore necessary, as President Reagan was later to put it, for "America to be able to walk tall again".

Reflecting the predominant mood, Congress gave approval to virtually all the military budget requests. The Administration lias been granted 97.5 per cent of the

US military spending 1946–1990
The military budget of the Reagan Administration will, on present projections, by 1990 have taken the level of peace-time spending up to the level reached at the end of World War II.

funding it demanded when it first set up the rearmament programme in 1981. In the intervening years the public mood has shifted somewhat, and Congress has become progressively more obstructive. But it will be difficult for Congress to reduce planned expenditures. There is a backlog of $243 billion in approved funds still waiting to be spent. Moreover, many of the major weapon programmes have reached a point at which the costs of cancellation could well equal or even exceed the costs of continuing. In any case, any attempt to cancel such programmes would be certain to evoke strong opposition from politicians and communities that have benefited from the substantial investment involved. There seems no immediate likelihood that Congress will be able to bring US military expenditure under control.

Spending on weapon procurement (particularly on strategic weapons) and spending on research and development have been the fastest-growing elements in the rearmament programme. Up till now, all the major strategic nuclear weapon programmes have been approved. Only one such programme—that for the MX missile—had some difficulty in getting Congressional approval. However, the Administration argued that the United States should not show weakness in the Geneva negotiations. This argument proved persuasive. In March 1985 the Senate and the House of Representatives, by a narrow majority, approved the release of $1.5 billion from the 1985 budget for the production of 21 MX missiles.

During 1984, Congress demanded evidence that the Administration was entering into meaningful negotiations with the Soviet Union, and wanted to know the Administration's plans for the modernization of European theatre nuclear forces and for reducing dependence on short-range battlefield nuclear weapons in Europe.

Most Air Force programmes (including cruise missile, B-1 bomber and F-16 fighter programmes) got through relatively unscathed. Similarly, the Navy's budget grew considerably, with programmes for new cruisers, nuclear attack submarines, the new Trident submarine and fighter aircraft going through. The Army too got its money for M-1 battle tank development, an attack helicopter and the Patriot air defence missile system. Hardly any weapon programmes were deleted; rather procurement (purchasing) of weapon systems was simply slowed down.

Acting upon numerous reports of scandalous overcharging such as $436 for claw-hammers and $9 600 for Allen wrenches, Congress took action to cut down on waste in weapon purchasing, calling for more competition and fairer pricing and for the Department of Defense to test and evaluate weapon systems itself rather than leave it to the manufacturers.

Coffee brewer
There are many examples of profligate spending by the Pentagon. In one case, several hundred coffee brewers were bought for $7 622 each although they were available in the shops for only $99.50. Justifying the purchase, a Pentagon spokesman said: "The brewer, which contains 2 000 parts, makes ten cups of coffee and is to be installed in the Lockheed C5A. It is a very reliable device and will continue making coffee after loss of cabin pressure following a direct hit".

Leaked reports from the Pentagon suggested that the readiness for action of the Army and Air Force had declined since 1980. In July 1984 a survey of military readiness by a Congressional subcommittee revealed that the Army did not have the men and material to sustain combat operations in a major emergency and that the Navy could not sustain a full-scale war with the Soviet Union beyond one week.

This was an ironic admission after several years of the largest ever peace-time military build-up, and at a time when defence spending showed signs of spiralling out of control because the costs of many weapon systems had been grossly underestimated. A number of people put this down to an overconcentration on weapon hardware to the exclusion of training, operation and maintenance.

During 1984, the US Congress expressed concern that the European allies were not carrying a fair share of defence costs. During 1984 a proposal in the US Senate which could have reduced US troops in Europe by 30 000 a year for three years was narrowly defeated. The proposal suggested that unless the European nations kept to the 3 per cent target increase or at least increased ammunition war-reserves to 30 days and improved air base facilities for US reinforcements to Europe, the USA should show its displeasure by scaling down its own contribution. The European countries did not see the problem in the same way: they were worried about the large proportion of their weapon spending which went to US manufacturers.

The NATO spending pattern

Military spending in the rest of NATO has not followed the US pattern. This reflects a different perception of the threat posed by the Soviet Union.

Military expenditure in NATO European countries has been rising by about 2 per cent a year in the 1980s, though growth rates have been above average in Canada, Italy and the UK. Much of this spending reflects an agreed plan to strengthen NATO conventional forces especially in terms of their readiness for battle, speed of reinforcement and mobilization of reserves. General Bernard Rogers, Supreme Allied Commander Europe, has argued that NATO countries are still not spending enough. He has said that only by increasing military spending by 7 per cent a year above the rate of inflation could early reliance on battlefield nuclear weapons be avoided in a European conflict.

Apart from the USA, only three NATO countries have met the 3 per cent growth rate target set out for the Long Term Defence programme agreed in 1978. *Canada* is involved in large capital programmes such as refitting destroyers, refurbishing the Hercules transport fleet,

US Department of Defense

building frigates and buying new fighter aircraft. The number of military personnel is also likely to be increased. The *Italian* modernization programme for all three services, which began in 1975, has experienced both delays and increased costs, and so has had to be extended until 1990.

In the *United Kingdom* spending rose by 3 per cent above inflation in 1984; but plans for 1985–87 show first a standstill and then a slight decline, despite considerable commitments. Partly as a result of the Falklands/Malvinas War, naval force cuts decided in 1981 have not been made. The number of front-line aircraft will be increased by 15 per cent. The cost of the Trident nuclear missile programme has risen from £6 billion in 1980 to £10.7 billion in January 1985. Nearly half of the costs for this programme are for US parts and will have to be paid in dollars. Movements in the dollar-sterling exchange-rate have been largely responsible for the cost inflation.

Cost increases resulting from delays in the Nimrod Airborne Early Warning and Tornado multi-role combat aircraft, together with new programmes for mechanized combat vehicles and helicopters, for example, also put a

US Trident submarine
Britain's replacement for its ageing Polaris fleet will be the Trident II armed with D5 missiles. The Trident programme marks a significant upgrading of the UK's strategic capabilities. Each of the D5 missiles could carry 10 independently targeted and highly accurate warheads compared with only 2 (much less accurate) MRVs on a Polaris missile. The costs of the programme have risen dramatically over the last five years.

strain on the budget. Proposed cost savings by reforming management structures and by increasing competition in arms procurement seem unlikely to achieve the necessary savings. Reductions in the British defence programme seem inevitable.

In 1983 *France* adopted a military programme which emphasized improvements in nuclear forces, military equipment and research. But poor economic performance has subsequently forced cuts in this programme. Manpower levels will continue to decline, as planned. In *West Germany*, major procurement programmes for the late 1980s include tactical fighter aircraft, anti-tank helicopters, frigates, submarines and missiles. Ammunition purchases are being substantially increased.

Overall in NATO Europe, the rise in military spending is likely to be well below 3 per cent in future. Weapon programmes have grown at the expense of spending on personnel, operations and maintenance. It seems most unlikely that programme commitments in the future can be met with the funds currently allocated.

There has been a lot of debate recently about the possibility of introducing new conventional weapon systems which would use the latest technology to overwhelm a Warsaw Pact attack. The idea, which originated in the USA, has been greeted with scepticism in Europe where it is felt that such untried technologies will be very expensive, yet of doubtful effectiveness. European defence industries could be largely excluded from contracts because of the huge US lead in technology, and large-scale spending on high-technology weapons would, it is argued, be at the expense of basic conventional improvements and front-line defence.

Because of the cost advantages to be gained, there has been renewed interest in joint weapon production among European states. France and West Germany have agreed to co-operate on an anti-tank helicopter. France, West Germany, Italy, Spain and the UK have begun a feasibility study for a European Fighter Aircraft. Eight countries, including the USA, have embarked upon a feasibility study for the co-production of 100 frigates. The large size of current and future NATO weapon projects demands combined effort. Independent arms production is, however, seen as a way of reducing unemployment and of keeping up with new technologies. Consequently, countries are unwilling to change their existing production patterns.

Within the USA there is some support for the idea of co-production or at least some co-operation with the European allies as an incentive to them to increase their contribution to the 'common defence'. But, at the same time, the USA is reluctant to share the technology which such co-operation would require, fearing that it may reduce the technological lead which the USA currently enjoys or may even lead to leaks of technical know-how to the Soviet Union. Therefore, this is likely to be a continuing area of dispute between the allies.

The Soviet Union

Since 1970 the Soviet Union has been announcing a rouble figure for its defence spending which has been almost static. This figure is regarded as inaccurate by Western analysts. The level of military spending is probably high in relation to Soviet national income, though the annual rate of increase has been low in recent years. It is significant, therefore, that in 1984 the Soviet Union announced a massive 12 per cent increase for 1985.

In 1984 President Chernenko called for a strengthening of the country's defence capabilities, arguing that "we cannot ignore the growing aggressiveness of imperialism and its attempts to gain military advantage over the socialist community". This and similar announcements during the year can be seen as a declaration that the Soviet Union will not allow itself to lose what it perceives as a rough equality with the West. It is also a warning to the Soviet people that increased military spending must divert resources from social programmes.

US Department of Defense

Soviet T-74
A T-74 tank, sometimes referred to as the T-80, one of a range of recent additions to the Soviet Union's conventional weapon arsenal.

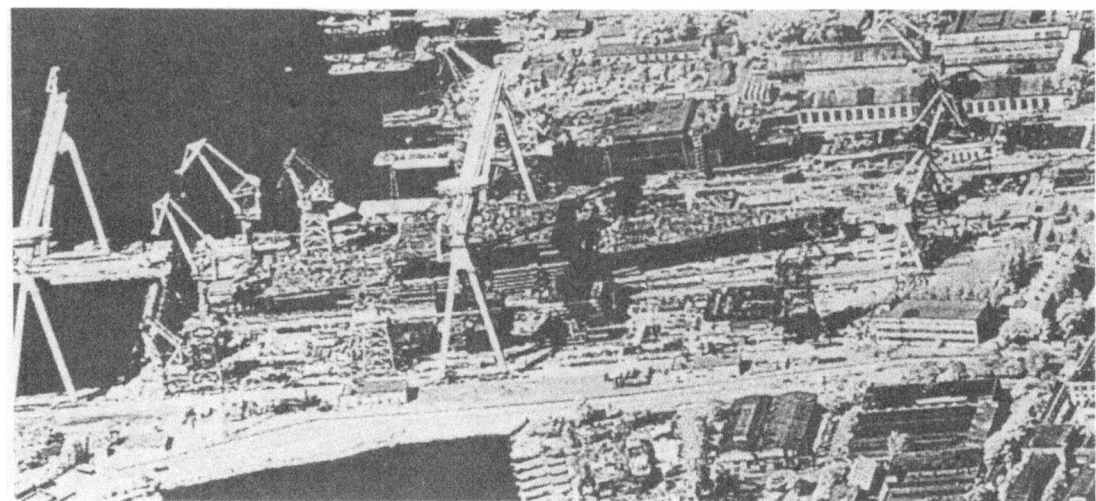

Spy photo of Soviet aircraft-carrier
A computer-enhanced satellite photograph of the Soviet Union's first large aircraft-carrier under construction in a Black Sea shipyard in 1984.

The US Department of Defense estimates that the Soviet Union is planning to introduce around 200 major new weapon systems in the coming years ranging from strategic nuclear systems to aircraft, ships and tactical missiles.

An increasing research investment is being made, especially in the field of electronics, where the Soviet Union has been particularly weak in the past. Some new ships have recently been put into service before their defensive electronic systems functioned while others have had to be modernized very shortly after delivery.

The Soviet Union lags well behind the USA in several areas including space weapons, air defence, tanks (where it still relies on the early T-72 and its derivatives) and ship construction (the Soviet Union's first big aircraft-carrier is still being built). But, if the recent pick-up in the Soviet economy continues in the future, we may expect to see a continuing growth in military spending.

China

China, for all its expressed concern about the Soviet threat, has placed military modernization last in its development programme behind industry, agriculture and science. Officially, the military have been receiving a declining share of the central budget since the war against Viet Nam, down from 16.0 per cent of the total budget in 1980 to 13.1 in 1984. In the same period, spending on culture, education, science and public health rose from 12.9 per cent of the budget to 17.2. However, official figures do not give the whole story of official spending: the budgeted amount does not include spending on research and development and major weapon systems.

China, while largely relying on its own efforts to modernize national defence, has recently been showing a greater interest in US and European weapons. China is keen to gain technical know-how because most of the systems it has are of Soviet 1950s vintage. China wishes to integrate Western components into its existing systems rather than to buy new systems outright. Military modernization is likely to remain slow for the foreseeable future, as foreign technology can only with difficulty be married to outmoded Soviet designs. Indeed, China can modernize its aircraft industry only if greater use is made of advanced technologies. A basic research programme to meet its own needs would be a very expensive enterprise to embark on at a time when there is an increasing demand for welfare and education programmes. China, under the Chairmanship of Deng Xiaoping, seems in the mood for wide-ranging innovation and change, although so far Chinese purchases from the West have been relatively modest.

Other parts of the world

Military spending in *South America* continued to decline from the very high levels of 1982 (the year of the Falklands/Malvinas conflict). Civilian governments have replaced military regimes in a number of countries but it has been hard for them to reduce the size and power of the military. Military spending in *Central America* is difficult to estimate though it is clearly fuelled by military aid from foreign sources. The level of domestic military spending of Costa Rica, Honduras, Nicaragua, El Salvador and Guatemala grew (on top of inflation) by a total of 60 per cent between 1979 and 1983. In 1983 their combined domestic budgets amounted to $880 million, while US security assistance in that year, to all but Nicaragua, amounted to $550 million.

In *South Asia* and the *Far East* military spending has grown more slowly after a peak in 1981 and 1982. India is seeking modern equipment for all three armed services, but a shortage of Western currency has obliged it to look once again to the Soviet Union for supplies, which the latter has been happy to provide. Japanese spending has risen at about 4 per cent annually in recent years, and is likely to reach 5.5 per cent in 1985. Such increases are putting additional pressure upon the ceiling of 1 per cent of GNP placed on military spending in the mid-1970s.

In the *Middle East* the figures for military spending in 1984 are not clear, particularly for Iran and Iraq. Military spending has, however, declined slightly among most other countries in the region. Egypt increased its military spending

Shanty dwellings in Peru
Many governments in the Third World spend a sizeable portion of their national income on the military. This is true even where the bulk of their citizens lack basic amenities such as decent housing, education and health care.

by 3 per cent in 1984, as well as receiving US military aid of $1 365 million. Israel, with an inflation rate in excess of 1 000 per cent, has had to make some cuts in 1984 and faces more in 1985. To offset these, Israel negotiated $2.6 billion in security aid from the USA for each of the years 1984 and 1985. This enabled Israel to devote more resources to military projects.

Three areas of present-day conflict

In times of conflict, the whole economy can be disrupted by the fighting. Official military spending figures are an inadequate measure of the real costs in terms of manpower and resources withdrawn from the economy and drafted into the war effort.

The aftermath of battle: near Basra in the Gulf War.

On the Thai–Kampuchean border, resistance to the Viet Nam-backed Kampuchean government continues.

In El Salvador the fortunes of the army and anti-government forces ebb and flow. The photograph shows a guerrilla assault on the city of Santa Rosa de Lima in the east of the country.

The trade in conventional arms

General trends

The general trend in the transfer of arms between countries has been downward since the early 1980s. The world recession has reduced the ability of many countries, particularly in the Third World, to pay for imported arms. Many of the latter are developing their own arms industries to substitute for imports. Also, many countries stocked up in the 1970s, and so only need to top up their stocks in the 1980s. But it is also becoming more difficult to detect arms transfers as it becomes more common to transfer spare parts, improvements and modifications rather than the whole systems which are counted in SIPRI estimates.

The arms trade has become a buyers' market and potential suppliers are having to work much harder and offer much more attractive deals to secure contracts than they tended to do in the 1970s. The USA is the main arms supplier with nearly 40 per cent of the world trade. During the period 1980–84 it supplied some 79 countries. The Soviet Union, with 32 per cent of the trade, currently supplies about 40 countries. The volume and share of Soviet weapons have declined sharply in the past few years. This may reflect Soviet unwillingness to part with high technology. It may also be because some Soviet weapons have not performed well. And, in at least a few cases (such as Libya and South Yemen), the recipients have all the weapons they can cope with. In terms of volume, NATO countries export twice as many weapons as do members of the Warsaw Pact.

The dominant position of the superpowers as arms suppliers to the Third World has declined substantially: from 79 per cent in 1980 to 53 per cent in 1984. Third World nations (which receive two-thirds of the arms transfers) have increasingly been choosing weapons from France, Italy, West Germany and from other Third World countries. The largest Third World importers are Egypt, Syria, Iraq, India, Libya and Saudi Arabia. Third World exporters, led by Brazil, Egypt and Israel, now account for about 3 per cent of the world arms trade.

The suppliers

The Soviet Union and other socialist countries
Arms exports, which in 1983 amounted to just over half of all Soviet exports to non-socialist countries in the Third World, earn valuable hard currency for the Soviet Union. In 1984 the Soviet Union's major customers—India, Iraq and Syria—bought a range of aircraft, tanks and missiles. Jordan, Kuwait and Nigeria also made purchases.

The decisions of Jordan and Kuwait to buy from the Soviet Union are interesting because they are usually regarded as Western customers. They bought Soviet equipment because the USA refused to sell them the advanced Stinger surface-to-air missile. This is one example of the declining ability of the major arms suppliers to influence what arms go where. Buyers are keen to get the most advanced technology. The Soviet Union has, for instance, sold the advanced MiG-29 to India even before it had been supplied to its own forces. If countries are refused, they may turn elsewhere.

Czechoslovakia, *Romania* and *Yugoslavia* are also significant arms exporters, producing their own weapon systems and re-exporting Soviet equipment, mainly to Third World countries.

Arms exporters, 1980–84
The USA and the Soviet Union together account for over 70 per cent of world sales of major weapons. But Third World countries like Israel and Brazil have now become significant weapon producers and exporters in their own right.

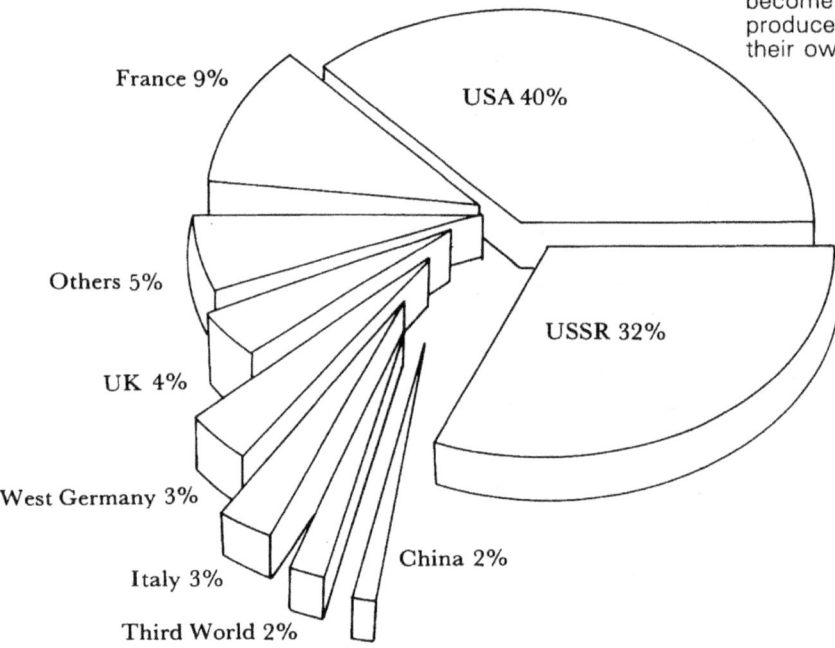

70

The People's Republic of China has recently entered the market as a serious arms exporter. In 1984 it took part in arms exhibitions and advertising which emphasized the reliability and cheapness of Chinese equipment. This change in Chinese policy is part of a wider effort to gain access to Western technology through barter agreements, industrial offsets and contracts which earn Western currencies.

North Korea too has reportedly become a major arms exporter, progressing in the 1980s from small arms supplier to supplier of major weapons; though these may be of doubtful quality since the Iranians are reported to have stopped their imports from North Korea and to have even returned some shipments.

The United States

The USA is the world's foremost supplier of arms. Arms sales are a key instrument of its foreign policy, supplied primarily to its allies and to support 'friendly' governments in key areas of international conflict. Under President Reagan, there have been far fewer restrictions on arms sales (both in terms of the range of arms available and the countries allowed to receive them) than existed during the Carter Administration.

Main arms importing regions, 1980–84
Nearly a third of all exports of major weapons goes to the poorest nations of the world. Another third goes to the conflict-torn Middle East. *Note:* The Far East excludes Japan and China. They are included amongst the group of industrialized countries.

- Industrialized countries 34%
- Middle East 33%
- North Africa 7%
- South Asia 7%
- Far East 6%
- Latin America 6%
- Sub-Saharan Africa 4%
- Central America 3%

In 1984 the USA encountered continued resistance to its policy of trying to sell to Third World countries jet fighters which do not incorporate the most advanced technology. The ability of potential buyers to shop around and their unwillingness to accept what they think are inferior-quality goods have led to the failure of this policy. Thus, it is hardly surprising that, among the 1 100 jet fighters sold by the USA to countries such as Egypt, Greece, Pakistan, Turkey and Saudi Arabia, there have been no sales of the cheaper US fighter specifically designed for Third World countries. Of these 1 100 planes, some 400 have been the advanced—and expensive—F-15s and F-16s.

During 1984 US arms producers concluded that China might become a massive market. The liberalization of trade between the USA and China was reflected in an increase in the value of the trade between them in high-technology items from $350 million in 1982 to over $2 billion in 1984. The sales are mainly of high-technology items which have civil uses but can also have military applications. China's attitude to the United States will probably continue to be cautious, signalling a lack of trust in US policies and intentions, as long as the latter continues to supply arms to Taiwan.

Chinese Norinco advert
China has recently entered the arms market as a supplier, in 1984 taking part in international arms exhibitions for the first time. Adverts have appeared in Western trade magazines offering the type 54-1 howitzer as a simple, efficient and robust weapon that has proven itself in combat.

Since the arms market is gradually becoming more competitive and buyers have a greater choice of supplier, an increasing number of US deals are now incorporating an element of 'industrial offset' where, for example, the buyer gets a licence to produce spares and accessories locally. According to the US General Accounting Office, these kinds of deal may cost the US economy some $30 billion over the next five years; but they will no doubt continue because of the strategic importance of maintaining supplies to friendly governments.

West European countries

For *France*, 1984 was a mixed year. It concluded a major deal with Saudi Arabia for air defence missiles, and supplied several missile systems to other countries. But, as the result of competition and depressed demand, aircraft sales were down by 45 per cent in 1984 as compared with 1983. *Britain* tried unsuccessfully to conclude a major deal with Saudi Arabia for Tornado and Hawk aircraft. There was criticism both at home and from the USA over supplies sent to Iran. The *Italian* government criticized its (largely state-owned) arms industries for supplying weapons to conflict zones such as Iran and Iraq. Both the *Swedish* and *Swiss* governments had to take serious criticism because some arms exports were being re-exported to war zones such as the Middle East. The *West German* government further reduced restrictions on sales to countries such as South Korea and Taiwan, both of whom were reportedly offered submarines.

Afghan guerrilla carrying a Kalashnikov rifle
In time of war weapons may be supplied through strange routes. Large numbers of Soviet Kalashnikov rifles have been supplied to the resistance fighters in Afghanistan through Pakistan, Egypt and other countries, paid for with money from Saudi Arabia and the USA. Greater numbers of weapons, however, have been captured from Soviet and Afghan soldiers or have been brought over by deserters.

The problem of the re-routing of arms sales from one destination to another is a serious one which governments find hard to control. In March 1984 customs officers in Minneapolis seized a $7 million consignment of tank parts destined for Iran. In order to avoid detection, the crates were labelled "automotive parts". To get to Iran they would have gone by rail to Montreal in Canada, and then by sea to Europe. They would have been transported across Europe to Austria and then on to Iran. This shipment was discovered; there are many more which are not.

The changing pattern of arms trade

1984 was a difficult year for most arms exporters. The world economic recession had reduced the demand for weapons while at the same time there were more countries with arms industries anxious to carve out an export market. Increasingly, export deals have had to carry industrial offset agreements as sweeteners. The value of the offset agreement may be several times greater than the arms deal itself.

Technology transfers may involve joint production of a weapon, or licensed production of the weapon or of components or spares for it in the buying country. Industrial offset agreements might give the buyer the right to market the weapon on behalf of the supplier and to offer maintenance contracts to other users of the weapon, or the arms supplier may agree to buy a range of other industrial goods from the customer in exchange for the arms contract.

The importance of the offset agreement can be illustrated by the example of the Belgian purchase in 1984 of 2 500 four-wheeled drive military vehicles. Canada won the order, in competition with British and West German suppliers, and an offset agreement worth three times the value of the arms contract itself helps to explain why. Canada will buy a substantial amount of arms from Belgian producers and will give about the same amount of business to vehicle producers in Belgium, with further guaranteed orders for other Belgian manufacturers. In addition, the vehicle will actually be assembled in Belgium. The Canada–Belgium offset agreement is increasingly typical of the package which has to accompany any substantial arms deal in today's competitive arms market.

Governments, particularly of the smaller arms exporting countries, are willing to underwrite such deals because they are desperate for the orders which are necessary to sustain their domestic arms production industries. Export sales are crucial for reducing the spiralling costs of arms production and for maintaining employment at home. The profitability of arms production is thus subsidized by the taxpayer, especially in Western Europe where the trend towards elaborate offset deals is strongest.

Even amidst this scramble for orders, the main suppliers still try to exercise some degree of control—though they often fail. The USA initially denied F-16s to Thailand and F-5Es to Honduras, mainly on the grounds that they would have upset the military balance in the area. (However, in 1985, Thailand's request was approved by the US government.) Similarly the Soviet Union refrained from supplying MiGs to Nicaragua. But many countries are able to circumvent such efforts at control simply by turning to other sources of supply, as Kuwait and Jordan did.

But there is also evidence that the controls on arms transfers which were painfully developed in the 1970s are being eroded. The behaviour of the superpowers plays a part in this. In 1981 the USA sold advanced F-16s to South Korea; in 1984 North Korea placed an order for the MiG-23, an advanced Soviet fighter.

One of the consequences of the indiscriminate supply of arms to a wide range of countries is that the suppliers occasionally find themselves being attacked with weapons originally supplied by themselves or by their allies. British forces experienced this during the Falklands/Malvinas conflict in 1982 when Argentina employed aircraft, helicopters, missiles and radar which Britain had previously supplied. Several British ships were damaged by missiles supplied by France which were fired from aircraft also supplied by France.

Gulf tanker
During 1984 Iraqi aircraft, using French-supplied Exocet missiles, damaged several tankers carrying Iranian oil from Kharg Island in the Persian Gulf. It is ironic that oil tankers, owned by or bound for the industrialized countries, are being attacked and damaged by missiles, bombs, aircraft and warships which have been delivered to Iraq and Iran by the very same industrialized countries.

Defence Attaché

More recently, in the war between Iraq and Iran, ships carrying oil from Iranian terminals to supply Western countries have been attacked by Exocet missiles which Iraq had bought from France. The Iraq–Iran War, now in its fifth year, has been deplored by many countries. But the fighting can only be sustained by the continued resupply of arms to the combatants. The USA, the Soviet Union, France, Italy and East Germany supplied major weapons to *both* sides in the period 1980–83.

Given the pressure upon the arms supplying countries to maintain their exports, it is probable that, as the world economy recovers and Third World countries have more money to spend, the trend of arms transfers will once again be upwards.

Nuclear arms control: hitting a moving target

An end to nuclear arms control?

After a long period of public hostility during which there were hardly any high-level contacts, the USA and the Soviet Union are at least talking to each other about nuclear weapons and space weapons. But while these negotiations are going on, big rearmament programmes are also in progress. This makes negotiations much more difficult. The negotiators have, as it were, to aim at a constantly moving target.

New missiles are being developed and deployed: on land, at sea and in the air. They are much more accurate than the old missiles they are replacing. Further, many of them are based in forward positions, near the borders of the other side. That makes them particularly dangerous. We are in the midst of a nuclear arms race of considerable proportions.

The fact that a very large research programme into defensive weapons is now beginning does not, unfortunately, make things better. If the USA does succeed, in the long run, in constructing some kind of defensive system, the Soviet Union is not likely to respond by reducing the number of its offensive weapons. The opposite is more likely to happen.

Indeed, viewed against the unprecedented peace-time military build-up taking place in the USA, it is difficult to accept at face value its declared intentions to negotiate in Geneva for deep cuts in offensive nuclear weapons. It is perhaps easier to see the advantages the Soviet Union could gain by achieving restraint in the nuclear competition in areas where it is at a particular technological disadvantage.

There are, of course, many motives behind the decision of the superpowers to sit around the negotiating table in Geneva. They wish to compete for political advantage. Geneva is a stage with a world audience. Neither adversary wishes to be regarded as 'the bad guy'. Furthermore, each is the leader of an alliance whose European members would benefit from eased relations between the superpowers. The consensus among NATO countries over security has been shattered by the nuclear deployments of the last few years. There are considerable bodies of domestic opinion in those countries that are deeply concerned about the current arms race. The European NATO governments cannot afford to ignore this strength of public opinion. They therefore have been pressing for negotiations between the USA and the Soviet Union. Thus, in comparison with other motives, the desire to negotiate meaningful arms control measures may, in reality, be low on the agenda in Geneva. The prospects for success do not, at present, look promising.

The negotiations could take a long time. Meanwhile, the existing treaties are beginning to fray at the edges. One treaty—the SALT I Interim Agreement—has expired; another—the SALT II Treaty—was never ratified by the USA. It is true that both sides say that they will continue to observe the main provisions of those treaties, but accusations are flying to and fro that the provisions are being infringed. It is possible that, before long, one side or the other might say that they do not regard themselves as bound by these treaties any longer. The one treaty which is properly in force is the Anti-Ballistic Missile Treaty. But if the research programme into ballistic missile defence goes much further, that treaty will either have to be renegotiated or abandoned.

What will other countries do if the USA and the Soviet Union proceed to some kind of unrestrained competition in nuclear weapons and in defensive weapons? Nearly 20 years ago, when a great many nations of the world undertook *not* to acquire nuclear weapons, the nuclear powers gave an undertaking that they would work in good faith towards nuclear disarmament. They have not done so. So far, the treaty which binds most of the nations in the world not to acquire nuclear weapons has held remarkably well. It may not continue to do so if the five nuclear weapon states go on adding to their nuclear weapon armouries without restraint.

Superpower image and security

Why do the superpowers continue with this competition in nuclear weapons? It is not for purely military purposes. On each side, the stock of nuclear weapons is now so large that no rational military purpose is served by adding to it further; people can be killed only once. One of the main reasons is this: both the United States and the Soviet Union are determined not to be seen to be inferior—and indeed both would like to be seen to be superior in some sense. Both believe that inferiority in some way damages their status in the world, and superiority enables them to 'walk tall'.

But although these weapons are not only being accumulated in pursuit of some kind of political machismo, the arsenals also grow through the sheer technological momentum of the military–industrial machine. Both

superpowers have created huge interlinked organizations which research, design and test new weapon systems. These complexes continually offer 'better' weapons, and most are eventually deployed. They also provide the threat assessments which underpin the decisions to deploy the symbols of political potency.

In fact, either superpower would gain far more by stopping than by continuing the relentless arms build-up. In the short run it would gain in status in the world; in the long run it would also gain in security. Suppose for a moment that either Mr Reagan or Mr Gorbachev were prepared to say: "We will stop all further nuclear weapon developments. We challenge the Soviet Union (or the United States, as the case may be) to do the same. Whatever the response, we will maintain the moratorium for a period of two years. We have enough nuclear weapons: we do not need any more. We consider it pointless to go on. That is our contribution to ending the nuclear arms race". A statement of this kind would enhance the political status of the country that made it, to a far greater extent than further additions to nuclear weapon stocks.

Some people are afraid that, if they urge their side to stop (whichever side that is), this will in some way make their side militarily weak. Once again, this is not the case. There is no military need to have the same number of nuclear weapons as the other side. The demand for 'parity' is a political demand, not a military one.

If the current nuclear arms competition could be stopped, there would be much more chance of success in the talks that are going on in Geneva. It makes very little sense to rearm in order to disarm. And if the talks lead eventually to reductions in the levels of nuclear weapon stocks, particularly those which are most threatening to the forces of the other side, that can only enhance the security of the superpowers. The superpowers cannot secure their long-term security by pursuing the nuclear arms race. Only negotiated agreements which restrain armaments and build mutual trust and confidence can do that. What then ought the priorities to be?

Steps towards nuclear disarmament

Arms control is not, of course, an end in itself. The aim is to avoid war—primarily nuclear war. Since it is unlikely that the nuclear powers will be willing (for the foreseeable future) simply to give up their nuclear weapons, the best way to avoid nuclear war is to establish, and then preserve, some kind of stable nuclear balance. Such a balance is virtually impossible to achieve in the midst of a massive rearmament programme. Thus, the first priority must be for the USA and the Soviet Union to observe some kind of mutual restraint while the talks are proceeding.

It happens that, at the present moment, the number of warheads deployed on each side are roughly equal, so a moratorium which halts all further deployments of strategic and intermediate-range weapons would meet political demands for parity. To this could be added a moratorium on testing space weapons and those which could be used for attacking objects in space.

Without some check of this kind, the chances of reaching an agreement are much reduced. Worse, the existence of negotiations could be used to justify further weapon developments in order to 'show resolve' or to use as a 'bargaining chip'. Such arguments were put forward in March 1985 as reasons why the US Congress should approve further funds for the MX programme. The logic of the bargaining chip argument has been shown to be false in past negotiations: new deployments are not negotiated away. But that does not stop such arguments being used and new systems being introduced even while talks are going on.

Negotiating priorities

What principles might be followed in the current negotiations in order to maximize the chances of reaching effective arms control agreements? It is good that both strategic and intermediate-range weapons are being discussed under one umbrella in Geneva because the distinction between the two levels is not always clear. Weapons with ranges of less than 5 500 km can be used for strategic missions if they are forward-based.

Offensive and defensive weapons also have to be considered together. Improvements in the defences of one side worsen the offensive capabilities of the other. With SDI on the horizon and the ABM Treaty under threat, it is very important that defensive systems have been included in negotiations.

Is it better to go for a comprehensive agreement, or a simpler, less ambitious one? One of the problems of trying for the former is that the complexities of a comprehensive agreement tend to slow down the pace of negotiations (as SALT II showed), and to centre the talks on the weapons of the past rather than on the technologies of the future (SALT II failed to consider the SLCM which is now deployed in such large numbers). Further, complex

Some suggestions for Geneva

The following steps would help to halt the arms race and improve the chances of successful negotiations:

- A temporary halt to nuclear weapon deployments during talks

- No testing of space weapons or of weapons aimed at objects in space

- Talk about defensive and offensive weapons at the same time

- Go for simple agreements that can be quickly achieved

- Try to get agreement on the most destabilizing weapons such as: the most accurate and vulnerable offensive weapon systems and forward-based systems

discussions may create ambiguities and verification problems. It may therefore be better to aim for an agreement which can be reached quickly and can lay the foundation for further agreements, even if it limits only a few dimensions of nuclear weapon capability. If the negotiators concentrated on limiting the numbers of deliverable warheads, that would be a feasible goal.

Alternatively, it would be productive to negotiate more elaborate provisions to discourage particular weapon systems, on the grounds that they are destabilizing. For example, the concentration of the early SALT talks on limiting the numbers of launchers encouraged the deployment of multiple warheads. This in turn made missile silos the main targets and led to a concurrent development of war-fighting strategies. Although it is now too late to undo these improvements in missile accuracy, if a ban on testing could also be negotiated, this might prevent further refinements being made.

The deployment of forward-based systems is also destabilizing. Because of the short flight-time to their targets, any warning of attack is correspondingly reduced. This increases the temptation, when a side believes itself to be under attack, to launch its retaliatory missiles on receiving the first warning of the attack. Such a response is most likely where offensive systems are both forward-based *and* themselves vulnerable to attack as are the Pershing II missiles in West Germany and the SS-12s and -22s in Eastern Europe. Forward deployment therefore encourages precipitate response in a crisis with all the possibilities of error or over-reaction that this entails.

Unfortunately, the USA and the Soviet Union have different perceptions about which systems are the most destabilizing. The US perception is that the accurate Soviet heavy missiles pose the greatest threat, while the Soviet Union argues that weapon systems which threaten its command, control, communications and intelligence (C^3I) facilities (such as Pershing II land-based missiles and Trident SLBMs) are the most destabilizing.

The negotiations about space weapons will clearly be one of the most difficult areas in Geneva. The US programme for ballistic missile defence is projected by those who support it as a stabilizing development. It is argued by those who see it as a defence of populations that it would be the adequacy of defence rather than the threat of retaliation that would prevent an attack from taking place. Others suggest that ballistic missile defence would enhance deterrence by providing defence for missile sites and command centres.

However, the SDI programme is being put forward at a time when the USA is engaged in a formidable programme

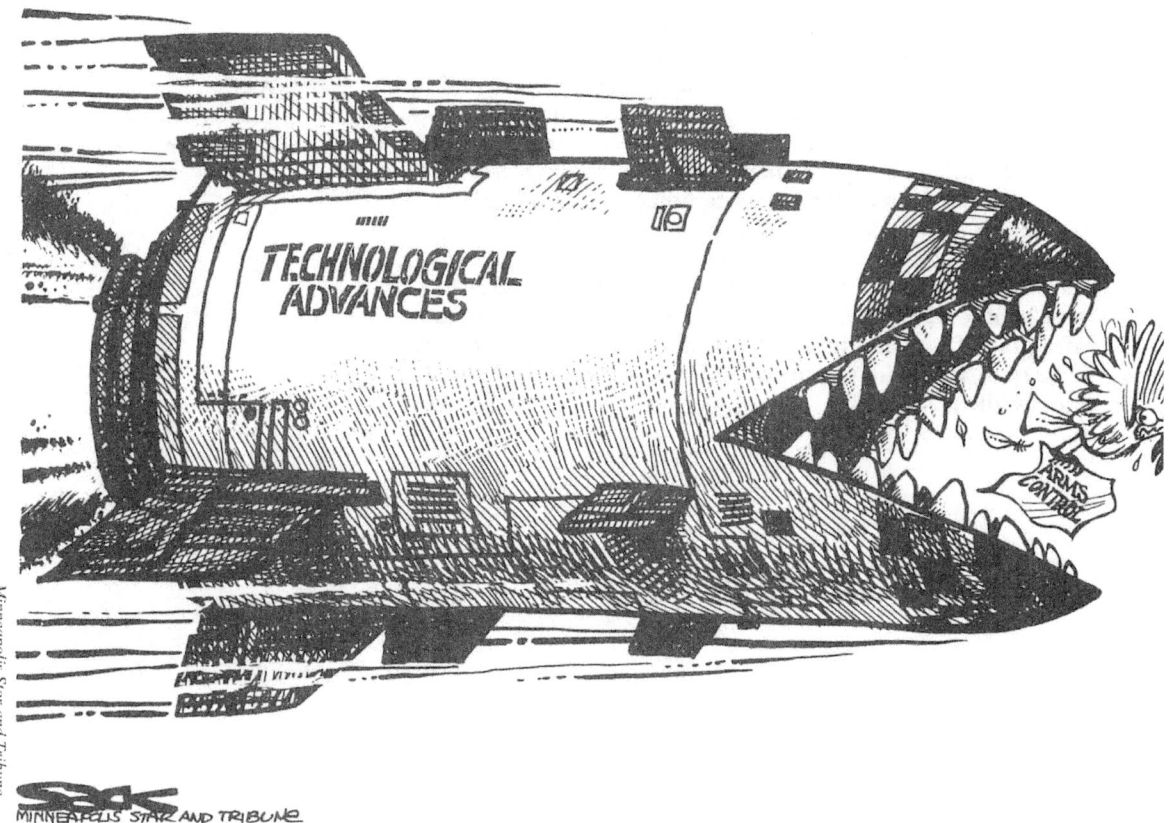

Minneapolis Star and Tribune

of strategic offence: all the missiles in the process of development and deployment have high degrees of accuracy. To the Soviet Union, this must appear as a programme for the development of war-fighting capabilities. If a ballistic missile defence is eventually added to the formidable array of offensive missiles, this would be seen as a part of a first-strike capability. The ballistic missile defence would be intended to deal with the retaliatory missiles left after a first strike. In this situation, SDI can be seen as extremely destabilizing.

The proponents of ballistic missile defence are contending that this new technological development will serve to stabilize the arms race in nuclear weapons. The experience of the past 40 years suggests that new developments in military technology have the opposite effect.

Throughout this book, the central role that technological change plays in shaping the arms race has been stressed time and time again. The new technologies of waging war must be curbed if the arms race is to be brought under control and put into reverse. It is not that technological innovations must necessarily be bad in themselves. But the new systems that are coming out of the arms machines of major military powers are almost always more threatening than the ones they replace. They are also deployed in ways which are increasingly threatening to the other side. In the arena of nuclear weapons, new technologies have made it possible for the first time to contemplate fighting and perhaps in some way 'winning' a nuclear war. The deployment of systems which are best suited to starting a nuclear war as part of a strategy of preventing one is the most profound contradiction. If the world is to be made a safer place from the threat of nuclear war, then the control of weapon technology must be the first and most urgent priority of negotiations.

SECTION III

Reference material

The material in this section is adapted from the *SIPRI Yearbook 1985*. It is intended to provide background details to the issues covered in the main text.

The information contained in the tables represents SIPRI estimates based upon the data available in published sources. Full details of the sources for the tables can be found in the *Yearbook*. Like all estimates of this kind, the tables should be treated with caution. Since published information on Warsaw Pact weapon systems is scant, and mainly based on intelligence estimates, figures in this area should be treated with even greater caution.

Where available data allows us to make only informed guesses, the tables either show an upper and lower range, or give the relevant figures in italics.

COMMON ABBREVIATIONS

AAM	Air-to-air missile
AASM	Advanced air-to-surface missile
ABM	Anti-ballistic missile
ACM	Advanced cruise missile
ALCM	Air-launched cruise missile
APC	Armoured personnel carrier
ASAT	Anti-satellite
ASM	Air-to-surface missile
ASMS	Advanced strategic missile system
ASW	Anti-submarine warfare
ATM	Anti-tank missile
AWACS	Airborne warning and control system
BMD	Ballistic missile defence
BW	Biological weapon
C^3I	Command, control, communications and intelligence
CBM	Confidence-building measure
CBW	Chemical and biological warfare
CD	Conference on Disarmament (Geneva)
CDE	Conference on Disarmament in Europe (Stockholm)
CEP	Circular error probable
COIN	Counterinsurgency
CSBM	Confidence- and security-building measure
CTB	Comprehensive test ban
CW	Chemical weapon
DC	Disarmament Commission
DoD	(US) Department of Defense
DoE	(US) Department of Energy
EMP	Electromagnetic pulse
Enmod	Environmental modification
ERW	Enhanced radiation (neutron) weapon
ET	Emerging technology
FBS	Forward-based systems
FEBA	Forward edge of the battle area
FOBS	Fractional orbital bombardment system
GLCM	Ground-launched cruise missile
IAEA	International Atomic Energy Agency
ICBM	Intercontinental ballistic missile
ICCM	Intercontinental cruise missile
ICJ	International Court of Justice
ICRC	International Committee of the Red Cross
INF	Intermediate-range nuclear force
IRBM	Intermediate-range ballistic missile
ISMA	International Satellite Monitoring Agency
Laser	Light amplification by stimulated emission of radiation
LOCPODs	Low-cost powered dispensers
LRTNF	Long-range theatre nuclear force
MAD	Mutual assured destruction
MARV	Manoeuvrable re-entry vehicle
M(B)FR	Mutual (balanced) force reduction
MBT	Main battle tank
MIRV	Multiple independently targetable re-entry vehicle
MLRS	Multiple launch rocket system

MRV	Multiple (but not independently targetable) re-entry vehicle
NATO	North Atlantic Treaty Organization
NGO	Non-governmental organization
NPT	Non-Proliferation Treaty
NWFZ	Nuclear weapon-free zone
PNE(T)	Peaceful Nuclear Explosions (Treaty)
PTB(T)	Partial Test Ban (Treaty)
R&D	Research and development
RDT&E	Research, development, testing and evaluation
RPV	Remotely piloted vehicle
RV	Re-entry vehicle
RW	Radiological weapon
SALT	Strategic arms limitation talks
SAM	Surface-to-air missile
SCC	Standing Consultative Commission (US–Soviet)
SDI	Strategic Defense Initiative
SLBM	Submarine-launched ballistic missile
SLCM	Sea-launched cruise missile
SRAM	Short-range attack missile
SRBM	Short-range ballistic missile
SSB	Ballistic missile-equipped, diesel-powered submarine
SSBN	Ballistic missile-equipped, nuclear-powered submarine
START	Strategic arms reduction talks
TOW	Tube-launched, optical, wire-guided
TTBT	Threshold Test Ban Treaty
VLS	Vertical launching system
WTO	Warsaw Treaty Organization (Warsaw Pact)

THE WORLD'S NUCLEAR FORCES

Notes

The figures in the nuclear weapon tables are estimates based upon a variety of official and unofficial sources. They give information on weapon systems. One should be very careful about using them to compare the military strengths of different countries. Military strength depends on many factors not included in these tables. Factors such as the reliability of the weapon systems, where they are deployed, how accurate they are, and how swiftly they could be used when needed are all important. Moreover, things such as the training and capability of military personnel, the geography of the adversaries and the military strategies employed will all have an influence upon the effectiveness of any particular weapon system.

US strategic nuclear forces, 1985

Delivery system	Weapon system Type	No. deployed	Year deployed	Range (km)	Warheads × yield	Warhead type	Number in stockpile
Land-based missiles	Minuteman II	450	1966	11 300	1 × 1.2 Mt	W-56	480
	Minuteman III	550	1970	13 000	3 × 170 kt/ 335 kt	W-62 W-78	825 1 000
	Titan II	30	1963	15 000	1 × 9 Mt	W-53	50
Submarine-based missiles	Poseidon	304	1971	4 600	10 × 40 kt	W-68	3 300
	Trident I	312	1979	7 400	8 × 100 kt	W-76	3 000
Bombers	B-52G/H	263	1955	16 000	8–24[a]	[a]	4 733
	FB-111	61	1969	4 700	6[a]	[a]	360
Aerial refuellers	KC-135	615	1957	—	—	—	—

[a] Bomber weapons include five different nuclear bomb designs with yields from 70 kt to 9 Mt, air-launched cruise missiles (ALCMs) with a yield of 200 kt, and short-range attack missiles (SRAMs) with a yield of 200 kt. FB-111s do not carry ALCMs or the 9-Mt bomb.

Soviet strategic nuclear forces, 1985

Delivery system	Weapon system Type	No. deployed	Year deployed	Range (km)	Warheads × yield	Number in stockpile[a]
Land-based missiles	SS-11 Mod 1[b]	520	1966	11 000	1 × 1 Mt	640–1 280
	Mod 2/3		1973		3 × 250–350 kt (MRV)	
	SS-13 Mod 2	60	1972	9 400	1 × 600–750 kt	60–120
	SS-17 Mod 3[c]	150	1979	10 000	4 × 750 kt	600–1 200
	SS-18 Mod 4	308	1979	11 000	10 × 550 kt	3 080–6 160
	SS-19 Mod 3[d]	360	1979	10 000	6 × 550 kt	2 160–4 320
Submarine-based missiles	SS-N-5	42	1963	1 400	1 × 1 Mt	42–60
	SS-N-6 Mod 1/2	336	1967	2 400	1 × 1 Mt	336–672
	Mod 3		1973	3 000	2 × 200–350 kt (MRV)	
	SS-N-8	292	1973	7 800	1 × 800 kt–1 Mt	292–584
	SS-N-17	12	1977	3 900	1 × 1 Mt	12–24
	SS-N-18 Mod 1/3	224	1978	6 500	3–7 × 200–500 kt	672–2 510
	Mod 2		1978	8 000	1 × 450 kt–1 Mt	
	SS-N-20	60	1983	8 300	6–9 × 350–500 kt	360–432
Bombers	Mya-4 Bison	45	1956	8 000	2 × bombs	90–180
	Tu-95 Bear	120	1956	8 300	2 × bombs and ASMs	366–812
	Tu-22M Backfire	130	1974	5 500	2 × bombs and ASMs	390–780
Aerial refuellers	[e]	125	—	—	—	—
ABMs	Galosh	32	1964	750	1 × 3–5 Mt	32–64

[a] Warheads represent low and high estimates of possible force loadings (including reloads).
[b] Approximately 100 Mod 1 with one warhead, 360 Mod 2, and 60 Mod 3 are deployed.
[c] Some SS-17 Mod 2 missiles with one warhead may also be deployed.
[d] Some SS-19 Mod 2 missiles with one warhead may also be deployed.
[e] Includes Badger and Bison A bomber converted for aerial refuelling.

US theatre nuclear forces, 1985

Delivery system	Weapon system Type	No. deployed	Year deployed	Range (km)	Warheads × yield	Warhead type	Number in stockpile
Aircraft	[a]	2 000	—	1 060–2 400	1–3 × bombs	[a]	2 800
Land-based missiles	Pershing II	54	1983	1 790	1 × 0.3–80 kt	W-85	54
	GLCM	80	1983	2 500	1 × 0.2–150 kt	W-84	100
	Pershing 1a	144	1962	740	1 × 60–400 kt	W-50	280
	Lance	100	1972	125	1 × 1–100 kt	W-70	1 282
	Honest John	24	1954	38	1 × 1–20 kt	W-31	200
	Nike Hercules	200	1958	160	1 × 1–20 kt	W-31	500
Artillery[b]	[b]	4 300	1956	30	1 × 0.1–12 kt	[b]	2 422
Atomic demolition mines	Medium/special	610	1964	—	1 × 0.01–15 kt	W-45/54	610
Naval systems							
Carrier aircraft	[c]	900	..	550–1 800	1–2 × bombs	[c]	1 000
Land-attack SLCMs	Tomahawk	50	1984	2 500	1 × 5–150 kt	W-80	50
ASW systems	ASROC	n.a.	1961	10	1 × 5–10 kt	W-44	574
	SUBROC	n.a.	1965	60	1 × 5–10 kt	W-55	285
	P-3/S-3/SH-3	630	1964	2 500	1 × <20 kt	B-57	897
Ship-to-air missiles	Terrier	n.a.	1956	35	1 × 1 kt	W-45	100

[a] Aircraft include Air Force F-4, F-16 and F-111, and NATO F-16, F-100, F-104 and Tornado. Bombs include four types with yields from 20 sub-kt to 1.45 Mt.
[b] There are two types of nuclear artillery (155-mm and 203-mm) with three different warheads: a 0.1-kt W-48, 155-mm shell; a 1–12-kt W-33, 203-mm shell; and a 1-kt W-79, enhanced-radiation, 203-mm shell.
[c] Aircraft include Navy A-6, A-7, F/A-18 and Marine Corps A-4, A-6 and AV-8B. Bombs include three types with yields from 20 kt to 1 Mt.

Soviet theatre nuclear forces, 1985

Delivery systems	Weapon system Type	No. deployed	Year deployed	Range (km)	Warheads × yield	Number in stockpile[a]
Aircraft	Tu-16 Badger	316	1955	4 800	2 × bombs and ASMs	632
	Tu-22 Blinder	139	1962	2 200	1 × bombs or ASMs	139
	Tactical aircraft[b]	2 545	—	700–1 000	1–2 × bombs	2 545
Land-based missiles	SS-20	396[c]	1977	5 000	3 × 150 kt	2 376
	SS-4	224	1959	2 000	1 × 1 Mt	224
	SS-12	120	1969	800	1 × 200 kt–1 Mt	120
	SS-22	100	1979	900	1 × 1 Mt	100
	Scud-B	570	1965	280	1 × 100–500 kt	1 140
	SS-23	48	1982	350	1 × 100 kt	48
	Frog	620	1965	70	1 × 10–200 kt	2 480
	SS-21	120	1978	120	1 × 20–100 kt	480
	SS-C-1B[d]	100	1962	450	1 × 50–200 kt	100
	[e]	n.a.	1956	40–300	1 × low kt	n.a.
Artillery	[f]	1 080	1974	10–30	1 × low kt	1 080
Atomic demolition mines	n.a.	n.a.	n.a.	—	n.a.	n.a.
Naval systems						
Aircraft	Tu-22M Backfire	105	1974	5 500	2 × bombs or ASMs	210
	Tu-16 Badger	240	1961	4 800	1–2 × bombs or ASMs	480
	Tu-22 Blinder	35	1962	2 200	1 × bombs	35
	ASW aircraft[g]	200			1 × depth bombs	200
Anti-ship cruise missiles	SS-N-3	336	1962	450	1 × 350 kt	336
	SS-N-7	96	1968	56	1 × 200 kt	96
	SS-N-9	200	1968	280	1 × 200 kt	200
	SS-N-12	136	1976	500	1 × 350 kt	136
	SS-N-19	88	1980	460	1 × 500 kt	88
	SS-N-22	36	1981	110	1 × ? kt	36
ASW missiles and torpedoes	SS-N-14	310	1968	50	1 × low kt	310
	SS-N-15	76	1972	40	1 × 10 kt	76
	SUW-N-1	10	1967	30	1 × 5 kt	10
	Torpedoes	n.a.	1957	16	1 × low kt	n.a.
Ship-to-air missiles	SA-N-6	264	1977	55	1 × low kt	264

[a] Estimates of total warheads are based on minimal loadings of delivery systems.
[b] Nuclear-capable tactical aircraft models include Su-24 Fencer, Su-17 Fitter, MiG-27 Flogger, MiG-21 Fishbed, Yak-28 Brewer, MiG-25 Foxbat and Su-25 Frogfoot.
[c] The Soviet Union denies that the figure is as high as this.
[d] Land-based anti-ship missile.
[e] Land-based surface-to-air missiles. Nuclear-capable SAMs probably include SA-1, SA-2, SA-5 and SA-10.
[f] Artillery includes 152-mm towed and self-propelled guns and 180-mm, 203-mm and 240-mm calibres.
[g] Includes Bear, Mail and May aircraft.

Major US nuclear weapon system development programmes

Weapon system	Total no. to be produced	First year operational	Spent by FY 1986 ($ bn)	Requested funding FY 1986 ($ bn)	Number requested	Proposed funding FY 1987 ($ bn)	Unit cost FY 1986 ($ mn)	Estimated total cost[a] ($ bn)	Comments
MX missile	223	1986	13.1[b]	4.0	48	3.2	116	25.9	100 deployed by 1989
Trident submarine	20–25	1982	16.8	2.0	1	1.8[c]	1 600	31–39	Cost for first 16 subs: $25.1 bn
Trident I	595	1979	8.1	0.066	0	0.047	19	11.2	For 12 Poseidon and 8 Trident, 211 tests and spares
Trident II	764	1989	4.4	2.7	0	3.6	49	37.4	For 16 subs; for 20–25, cost would be $42–48 bn
B-1B	100	1986	26.4	6.0	48	0.136	400	40	90 operational aircraft
Stealth	132	1990s	[d]	0.80	0	2.272	?	40–50?	One estimate $6.3 bn for FY 84–88
B-52 modifications	263	Ongoing	3.3	0.480	—	0.805	20 each	5.8	Radar, engines, avionics
ALCM	1 739	1982	4.1	0.049	0	0.037	2.5	4.5	Production stopped
GLCM	565	1983	2.8	0.620	95	0.243[c]	6.5	3.7	
SLCM	4 068	1984	3.3	0.849	249	1	3.2	13.0	758 nuclear versions
Advanced cruise missile	2 600	1988	?	?	0	?	5–7	7.0	Figures are estimates
Pershing II	325	1983	2.2	0.335	70	0.007	7.0	2.9	
Midgetman	1 000	1992	.807	0.625	0	?	38–70	38–70	20-year cost could be $107 bn

[a] Does not include DoE costs for nuclear warheads and bombs which normally are an additional 10–20 per cent of the weapon system cost.
[b] Does not include $1.5 billion for 21 missiles in FY 1985 budget pending Congressional vote.
[c] Does not include military construction funds.
[d] Partial figures first available in FY 1986 budget request are not comprehensive.

Soviet nuclear weapon systems introduced or under development, 1981–85

Strategic	Theatre/tactical
SS-18 Mod 5	SS-X-28 (replacement for SS-20)
SS-18 Mod 4	SS-21
SS-X-24	SS-22
SS-X-25	SS-23
SS-X-26	Replacement for SS-21
SS-X-27	Replacement for SS-22
SS-NX-23/Delta IV	Replacement for SS-23
New undesignated SLBM	SS-CX-4
Bear G	MiG-27 Flogger J
Bear H/with AS-15 ALCM	Su-25 Frogfoot
Blackjack A	152-mm howitzer M-1987
Backfire C	SS-N-21
ABM-X-3	SS-N-22
	Next-generation SLCM/GLCM

US European nuclear modernization, 1985–92

Weapon system (warhead)	As of 1985	Withdrawals[a]	As of 1992
Stored in Europe			
Pershing II	54	0	108
Pershing 1a	231	131	100
Ground-launched CM	100	0	464
Bombs	1 730	0	1 730
Lance	690	0	690
Honest John	190	190	0
Nike Hercules	680	680	0
8-inch (W-33)	930	500	430
8-inch (W-79)	0	0	200[b]
155-mm (W-48)	730	350	380
155-mm (W-82)	0	0	100
Atomic demolition mines	370	370	0
Depth bombs	190	0	190
Total in Europe	5 895	2 221	4 392
Committed to Europe[c]			
Poseidon	400	0	400
Carrier bombs	360	0	500
Bombs	600	0	800
Depth bombs	140	0	140
Lance	380	0	380
8-inch (W-79)	200	0	200
Total committed	2 080	0	2 420
Total	7 975	2 221	6 812

[a] Withdrawals in accordance with the modernization decision of 1979 (equal withdrawals for deployments); the Montebello decision of 1983 (1 400 additional withdrawals); and (other) anticipated changes in artillery stockpiles.
[b] Deployment of non-enhanced radiation warheads in Europe.
[c] Warheads committed by Europe or planned for storage in Europe (does not include tactical naval nuclear weapons).

Chinese nuclear forces, 1985

Delivery	Weapon system Type	No. deployed	Year deployed	Range (km)	Warheads × yield	No. in stockpile
Aircraft[a]	B-4 (Bull)	30	1966	6 100	1–4 × bombs	30
	B-5 (Beagle)	10	1974	1 850	1 × 1 Mt	10
	B-6 (Badger)	100	1966	5 900	1–3 × 1 Mt	30
Land-based missiles	CSS-1 (DF-2)	40–60	1966	1 100	1 × 20 kt	40–60
	CSS-2 (DF-3)	85–125	1972	2 600	1 × 2–3 Mt	85–125
	CSS-3 (DF-4)	~5	1978	7 000	1 × 1 Mt	10
	CSS-4 (DF-5)	~5	1980	12 000	1 × 5–10 Mt	10
	DF-1[b]	10–30	1966	650	1 × 2–10 kt	10–30
Submarine-based missiles	CSS-N-3	26	1983	3 300	1 × 200 kt–1 Mt	26

[a] All figures for these bomber aircraft refer to nuclear-capable versions only. Hundreds of these aircraft are also deployed in non-nuclear versions.
[b] A number of SRBMs (DF-1s) have been deployed in 'theatre support' roles, although they may no longer be active. Some of the MRBM and IRBM missiles are assigned to 'regional nuclear roles'. China has tested a number of warheads with yields from 2 to 20 kt.

French nuclear forces, 1985

Delivery system	Weapon system Type	No. deployed	Year deployed	Range (km)[a]	Warheads × yield	Warhead type	Number in stockpile
Aircraft[b]	Mirage IVA[b]	34	1964	1 560	2 × 70 kt	AN-22	75
	Jaguar A	45	1973	1 400	1 × 6–8/30 kt	[c]	50
	Mirage IIIE	30	1964	1 200	1 × 6–8/30 kt	[c]	35
Air refuellers	C-135F	11	1965	—	—	—	—
Land-based missiles	S3	18	1980	3 500	1 × 1 Mt	TN-61	18
	Pluton	42	1974	120	1 × 15–25 kt	ANT-51	120
Submarine-based missiles	M-20	80	1977	3 000	1 × 1 Mt	TN-61	80
	M-4	16	1985	4 000	6 × 150 kt	TN-70	96
Carrier aircraft	Super Etendard	36	1978	650	1 × 6–8/30 kt	[c]	40

[a] Range for aircraft indicates combat radius.
[b] The AN-51 warhead is also possibly a secondary bomb for tactical aircraft, and the AN-52 is also possibly a secondary bomb for the Mirage IVA.
[c] Warheads include ANT-51, ANT-52 and possibly a third type.

British nuclear forces, 1985

Delivery system	Weapon system Type	No. deployed	Year deployed	Range (km)[a]	Warheads × yield	No. in stockpile
Aircraft	Buccaneer 52[b]	30	1962	1 700	2 × bombs	60
	Jaguar A[b]	36	1973	1 400	1 × bombs	36
	Tornado GR-1[c]	140	1982	1 300	2 × bombs	280
Submarine-based missiles	Polaris A3	32	1968	4 600	3 × 200 kt	96
	Polaris A3-TK	32	1982	4 700	2 × 40 kt	64
Carrier aircraft	Sea Harrier	30	1980	450	1 × bombs	30
ASW helicopters	Sea King	69	1976	—	1 × depth bombs	69
	Wasp	16	1963	—	1 × depth bombs	16
	Lynx	35	1976	—	1 × depth bombs	35

[a] Range for aircraft indicates combat radius.
[b] Some Buccaneer and Jaguar aircraft withdrawn from bases in FR Germany may be assigned nuclear roles in the UK.
[c] 220 Tornado attack aircraft (GR-1) are on order for the Royal Air Force and continue to replace Jaguar aircraft.

Note: 34 Nimrod ASW aircraft, 12 Lance launchers and artillery guns also certified to use US nuclear weapons.

Nuclear explosions, 1945–84 (known and presumed)

Year	USA a	USA u	USSR a	USSR u	UK a	UK u	France a	France u	China a	China u	India a	India u	Total
16 Jul 1945–5 Aug 1963[a]		331		164		23		8		0		0	526
6 Aug–31 Dec 1963	0	14	0	0	0	0	0	1					15
1964	0	29	0	6	0	1	0	3	1	0			40
1965	0	28	0	9	0	1	0	4	1	0			43
1966	0	40	0	15	0	0	5	1	3	0			64
1967	0	28	0	15	0	0	3	0	2	0			48
1968	0	33[b]	0	13	0	0	5	0	1	0			52
1969	0	29	0	15	0	0	0	0	1	1			46
1970	0	30	0	12	0	0	8	0	1	0			51
1971	0	12	0	19	0	0	5	0	1	0			37
1972	0	8	0	22	0	0	3	0	2	0			35
1973	0	9	0	14	0	0	5	0	1	0			29
1974	0	7	0	19	0	1	7	0	1	0	0	1	36
1975	0	16	0	15	0	0.	0	2	0	1	0	0	34
1976	0	15	0	17	0	1	0	3	3	1	0	0	40
1977	0	12	0	16	0	0	0	6	1	0	0	0	35
1978	0	12	0	27	0	2	0	7	2	1	0	0	51
1979	0	14	0	29	0	1	0	9	0	0	0	0	53
1980	0	14	0	21	0	3	0	11	1	0	0	0	50
1981	0	16	0	21	0	1	0	11	0	0	0	0	49
1982	0	18[c]	0	31	0	1	0	5	0	0	0	0	55
1983	0	15	0	27	0	1	0	7	0	1	0	0	51
1984	0	15	0	27	0	2	0	7	0	2	0	0	53[d]
Total 6 Aug 1963–31 Dec 1984	0	414	0	390	0	15	41	77	22	7	0	1	967
Total	745		554		38		126		29		1		1 493

[a] 5 Aug 1963 was the date on which the Partial Test Ban Treaty was signed.
[b] Five devices used simultaneously in the same test are counted here as one explosion.
[c] Two devices used simultaneously in the same test are counted here as one explosion.
[d] The data for 1984 are preliminary.

a = atmospheric, u = underground.

US intelligence comparisons of Soviet and US chemical weapon stocks

CW posture element	USSR	USA
Protective capabilities		
Personnel dedicated to CW protective missions	85 000	7 000
Number of large mobile decontamination and reconnaissance devices	20 000[a]	1 000
Collective anti-CW protection installed in vehicles and ships	Yes	Few
Collective anti-CW protection installed in key facilities	Yes	Few
Deployment of reconnaissance vehicles for CW-agent detection and warning	Yes	No
Number of military chemical schools	4	1
Length of longest CW education/training course	5 years	6 months
Hours of formal chemical training per year	100–400	16–100
Number of field training areas	78	0[b]
Conduct of CW defence exercises	Yes	Yes
Offensive/retaliatory capabilities		
Number of different CW agents held	12, probably more	3[c]
Tonnage of CW agent held[d]	150 000–750 000[e]	Less than 50 000[f]
Deliverable CW munitions held[d]	80 times US holdings[g]	
CW-agent production facilities	14[h]	0[i]
Types of CW-agent delivery systems held:		
Landmines	Yes	Yes
Artillery and mortar	Yes	Yes
Multiple rocket launchers	Yes	No
Tactical rockets	Yes	No
Ballistic missiles	Yes	No
Aircraft bombs	Yes	Yes
Aircraft spraytanks	Yes	Yes
Air-to-ground rockets	Probably	No
Aircraft cluster-bombs	Yes	No

[a] 20 000–30 000 in the 1982 net assessment; 18 000–12 000 in the 1981.
[b] 1 in the 1982 net assessment.
[c] In fact, 6: GB, VX, HD, HT, plus as-yet-undestroyed stocks of the incapacitants DM and BZ.
[d] Figures, presumably from a Defense Department source, quoted on the floor of the Senate on 8 November 1983.
[e] The range of estimates quoted by the Defense Department in 1982 was 30 000 to 700 000 tons.
[f] A figure of 31 000 tons was quoted in 1982 by a former US official.
[g] In the view of US Air Force Intelligence, the USSR has "about 100 times more chemical munitions than the United States".
[h] In the view of US Air Force Intelligence, the USSR has "between 19 and 50 chemical munitions production plants".
[i] In fact, 3. They are all in standby status, requiring much restoration prior to reactivation.

World military spending 1975–84, summary table

Figures are in US$ billion, at 1980 prices and exchange rates.
Totals may not add up due to rounding.

	1975	1976	1977	1978	1979	1980	1981	1982	1983	1984
USA	139	132	137	138	139	144	154	168	180	200
Other NATO	100	102	103	107	109	112	113	116	119	122
Total NATO	239	233	240	245	248	256	267	284	299	322
USSR	*122*	*124*	*126*	*128*	*130*	*132*	*134*	*136*	*138*	*142*
Other Warsaw Pact	11	12	12	12	12	12	*13*	*13*	*14*	*14*
Total Warsaw Pact	*133*	*136*	*138*	*140*	*142*	*144*	*146*	*149*	*152*	*156*
Other Europe	13	14	14	14	15	15	15	16	16	*16*
Middle East	35	39	37	37	39	41	*46*	*50*	*46*	*46*
South Asia	5	6	6	6	6	7	7	8	8	8
Far East (excl. China)	*19*	*21*	*22*	*25*	*25*	*27*	*28*	*30*	*31*	*32*
China	37	38	36	41	53	43	36	38	37	36
Oceania	4	4	4	4	4	4	5	5	5	5
Africa (excl. Egypt)	12	13	13	14	15	*14*	*13*	*12*	*12*	*11*
Central America	2	2	2	2	2	2	3	3	3	3
South America	9	10	10	10	10	10	11	*16*	*14*	*13*
World total	**507**	**514**	**523**	**538**	**560**	**564**	**577**	**610**	**623**	**649**
Industrial market economies	258	253	260	266	271	280	290	308	324	349
Non-market economies	*172*	*175*	*177*	*183*	*198*	*190*	*185*	*190*	*192*	*196*
Major oil-exporting countries	33	37	*36*	38	39	42	*45*	*49*	*45*	*45*
Rest of the world	43	48	49	49	51	51	54	62	60	57
With 1982 per capita GNP:										
Less than US $440	7	7	7	8	8	8	9	10	10	10
Between US $440–1 680	9	9	10	9	9	8	8	9	9	9
Greater than US $1 680	28	31	32	33	35	35	37	43	41	39

Notes

(1) The figures in the table are in constant prices. They have been adjusted to remove the effects of inflation. The use of constant prices makes it possible to compare levels of spending at different points in time. When figures have been adjusted in this way, we often say that we are talking in 'real' terms.

The table has been constructed from figures for the military spending of 127 countries using the price levels that existed in 1980 as the basis for comparison. The figures have been converted from national currencies into dollars at 1980 exchange rates, and all figures are expressed in constant 1980 prices. Official exchange rates for the dollar are not used for China and the Soviet Union; rather, an attempt is made to assess the purchasing power of a dollar in these countries. For this reason, and because the military spending figures of these two countries are incomplete, SIPRI estimates are only very approximate.

(2) The figures in italics are uncertain or estimated data.

World military spending: annual rates of change, 1976–84

	1976	1977	1978	1979	1980	1981	1982	1983	1984
USA	−5.4	4.1	0.6	0.6	3.7	6.9	9.0	7.1	11.5
Other NATO	2.0	1.7	3.6	2.2	2.7	0.7	2.6	2.7	2.2
Total NATO	−2.3	3.0	1.9	1.3	3.3	4.2	6.3	5.3	7.8
USSR	*1.5*	*1.5*	*1.5*	*1.5*	*1.5*	*1.5*	*1.5*	*1.5*	*3.0*
Other Warsaw Pact	4.4	2.7	2.9	1.3	0.8	1.3	3.3	6.1	2.7
Total Warsaw Pact	*1.7*	*1.6*	*1.6*	*1.5*	*1.4*	*1.5*	*1.6*	*1.9*	*2.9*
Other Europe	4.7	−0.2	1.4	5.4	3.2	−0.6	2.8	2.2	0.2
Middle East	10.0	*−3.7*	*−0.4*	4.8	6.1	*11.5*	8.9	*−7.3*	*−0.4*
South Asia	13.4	*−3.4*	4.5	8.6	4.5	6.9	10.5	4.8	1.9
Far East (excl. China)	*9.2*	*7.4*	*10.2*	*3.9*	*5.1*	*5.9*	6.5	3.2	*1.5*
China	2.2	−3.7	11.9	30.1	−19.0	−15.7	4.7	−3.2	−0.8
Oceania	−0.4	0.4	1.8	3.0	5.9	7.2	4.0	0.9	3.8
Africa (excl. Egypt)	11.6	3.2	4.0	*6.2*	*−5.7*	*−9.2*	*−3.0*	*−2.4*	*−8.6*
Central America	13.9	27.0	6.5	7.3	0.0	8.6	*5.1*	*6.4*	*4.7*
South America	10.9	6.7	−1.0	0.0	1.5	3.0	48.0	−10.9	−7.5
World total	**1.3**	**1.8**	**2.7**	**4.2**	**0.7**	**2.2**	**5.7**	**2.1**	**4.2**
Industrial market economies	−1.9	3.0	2.1	1.9	3.5	3.7	6.0	5.3	7.5
Non-market economies	*1.9*	*0.7*	*3.8*	*7.9*	*−4.0*	*−2.3*	*2.3*	*1.0*	*2.3*

Note
The figures in the table show the annual real growth or decline in military spending. Although the growth in any one year may be small, the growth is cumulative, i.e., each year's growth adds to last year's growth. Thus, for example, the growth of total world military spending for the whole ten-year period is 28 per cent. The figures in italics are uncertain or estimated data.

The leading major-weapon exporting countries, 1980–84

Country	1980	1981	1982	1983	1984	1980–84
USA	5 577	5 559	6 186	5 655	4 685	27 662
	36.7	**38.5**	**42.9**	**40.1**	**40.4**	**39.7**
USSR	6 538	4 741	4 184	4 174	2 532	22 170
	43.1	**32.9**	**29.0**	**29.6**	**21.9**	**31.8**
France	1 144	1 347	1 241	1 360	1 242	6 335
	7.5	**9.3**	**8.6**	**9.7**	**10.7**	**9.1**
UK	431	532	667	519	822	2 972
	2.8	**3.7**	**4.6**	**3.7**	**7.1**	**4.3**
FR Germany	316	435	250	613	746	2 359
	2.1	**3.0**	**1.7**	**4.4**	**6.4**	**3.4**
Italy	366	531	576	374	372	2 219
	2.4	**3.7**	**4.0**	**2.7**	**3.2**	**3.2**
Third World	192	306	438	467	311	1 714
	1.3	**2.1**	**3.0**	**3.3**	**2.7**	**2.5**
China	82	148	221	222	430	1 103
	0.5	**1.0**	**1.5**	**1.6**	**3.7**	**1.6**
Others	533	831	668	707	444	3 182
	3.5	**5.8**	**4.6**	**5.0**	**3.8**	**4.6**
Total	15 179	14 430	12 431	14 091	11 584	69 715

Figures for amounts are in US$ millions at 1975 prices.
Figures in bold are percentage shares of world exports.
Figures may not add up to totals due to rounding.

Note

The term 'major weapons' refers to aircraft, armoured vehicles, heavy artillery, missiles and warships. The SIPRI prices are indexes based on military-use value and production costs. They do not correspond to the actual prices paid which would often be impossible to determine. The table shows, for example, that the USA delivered $5 577 million worth of major weapons in 1980: this equals 36.7 per cent of all arms transfers during that year. Similarly, Chinese deliveries during the period 1980–84 amounted to $1 103 million, or 1.6 per cent of global arms sales during these five years.

Exports of major weapons to the Third World, 1975–84

The USA is now once again the biggest exporter of major weapons to the Third World. The share of the European exporters is growing.

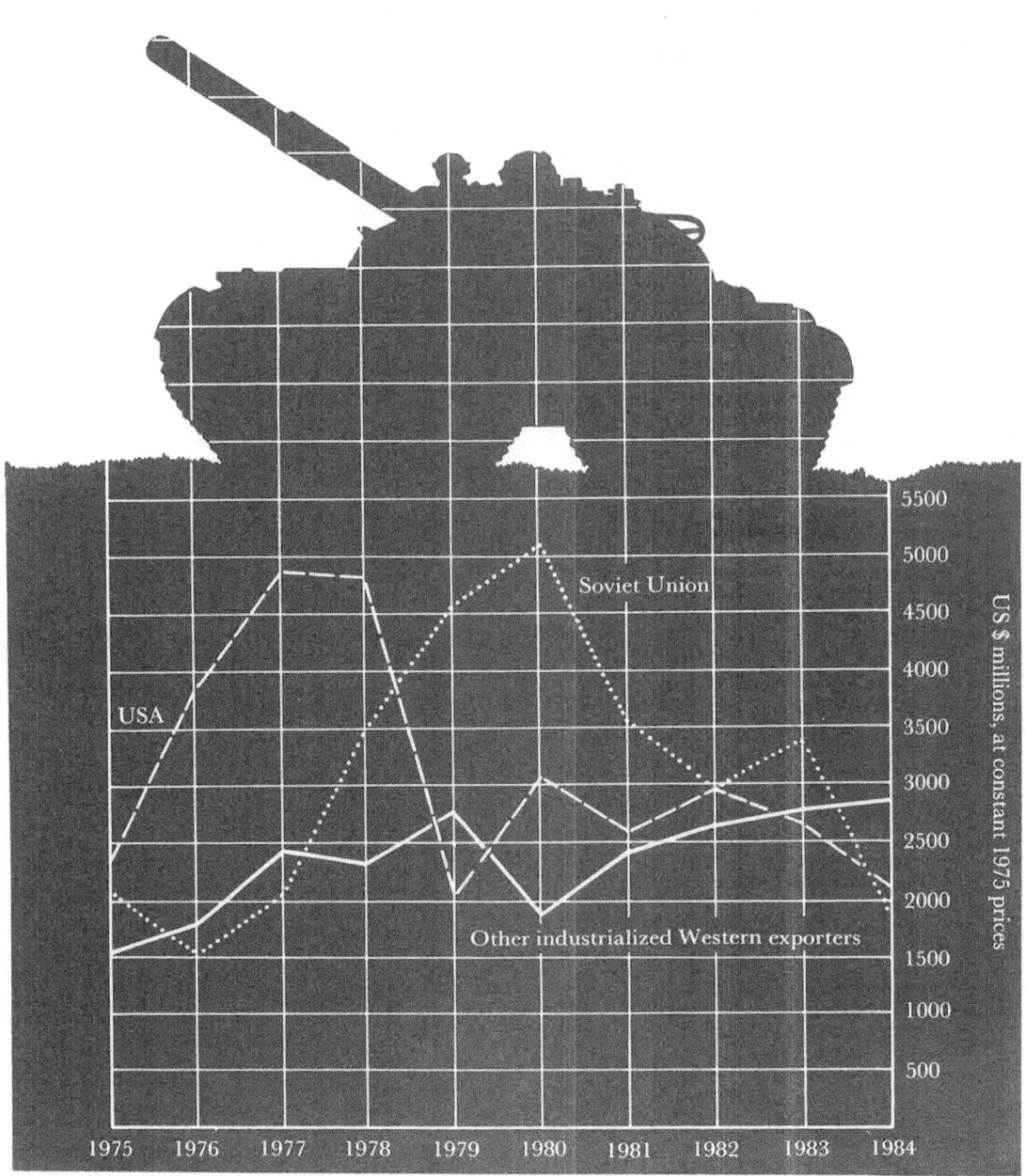

Imports of major weapons: by region, 1975–84

The figures for the *Middle East* include Egypt. About 60 per cent of the figures for *Africa* are accounted for by the four North African countries Algeria, Libya, Morocco and Tunisia. Cuba and Argentina are the largest arms importers in *Latin America*; they take about 50 per cent of the region's import of major weapons during 1980–84. The *Far East*, sometimes also referred to as South-East Asia or East Asia, includes arms imports by the small island nations in the Pacific (Oceania) and excludes arms imports by China and Japan.

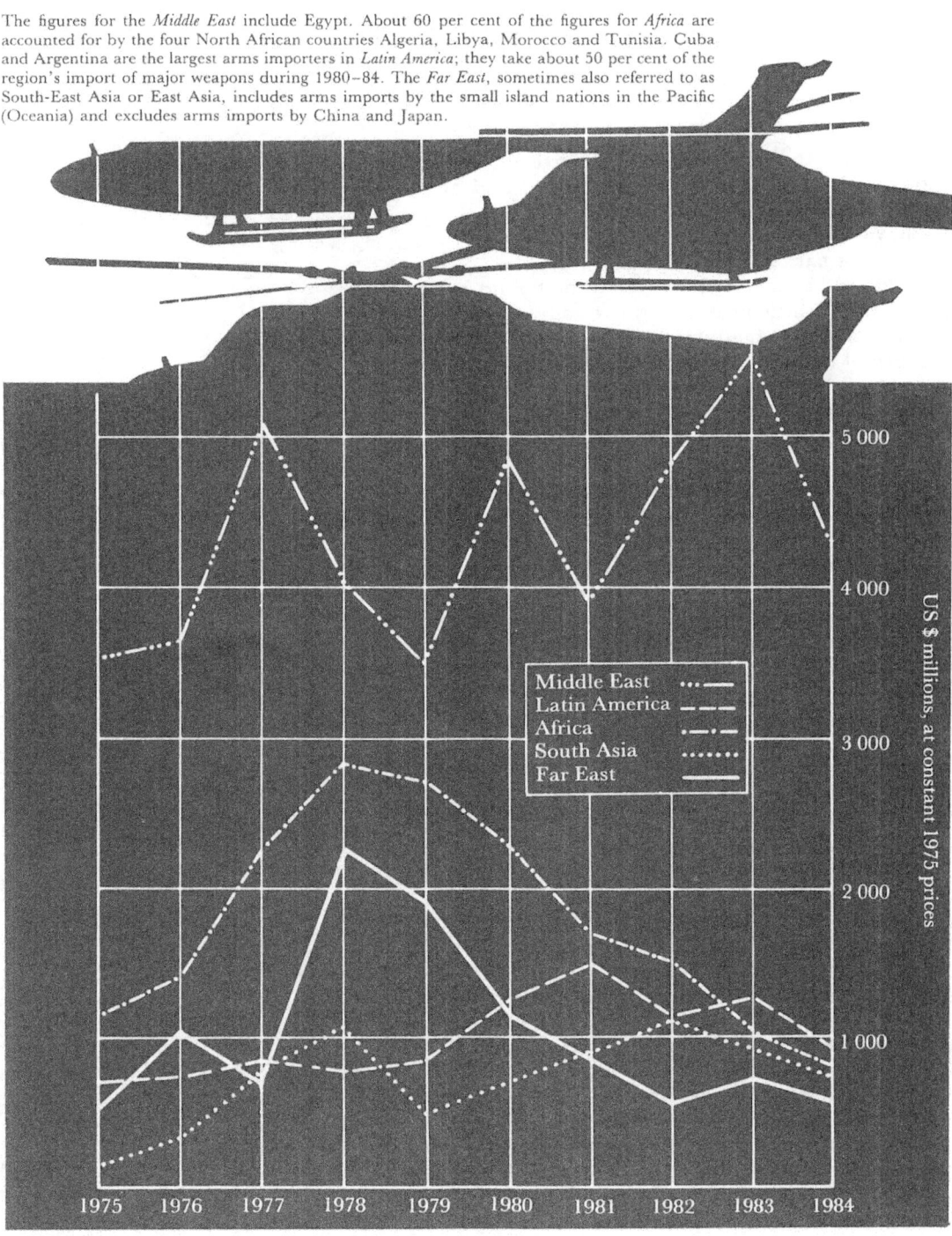

MULTILATERAL ARMS CONTROL AGREEMENTS

Brief descriptions of the agreements
The agreements are listed in chronological order. The status of their implementation is as of 31 December 1984.

Protocol for the prohibition of the use in war of asphyxiating, poisonous or other gases, and of bacteriological methods of warfare (Geneva Protocol), *1925*
Number of parties: 106.

Declares that the parties agree to be bound by the above prohibition, which should be universally accepted as part of international law, binding alike the conscience and the practice of nations. (Reservations made by a number of states have limited the applicability of the Protocol to nations party to it and to first use only.)

Conventions for the protection of war victims (Geneva Conventions), *1949*
Number of parties: 161.

Convention (I) provides for the amelioration of the condition of the wounded and sick in armed forces in the field.

Convention (II) provides for the amelioration of the condition of the wounded, sick and shipwrecked members of armed forces at sea.

Convention (III) is relative to the treatment of prisoners of war.

Convention (IV) is relative to the protection of civilian persons in time of war.

Antarctic Treaty, *1959*
Number of parties: 31.

Declares the Antarctic an area to be used exclusively for peaceful purposes. Prohibits any measure of a military nature in the Antarctic, such as the establishment of military bases and fortifications, and the carrying out of military manoeuvres or the testing of any type of weapon. Bans any nuclear explosion as well as the disposal of radioactive waste material in Antarctica, subject to possible future international agreements on these subjects.

Representatives of the contracting parties meet at regular intervals to exchange information and consult each other on matters of common interest pertaining to Antarctica, as well as to recommend to their governments measures in furtherance of the principles and objectives of the Treaty.

**Treaty banning nuclear weapon tests in the atmosphere, in outer space and under water
(Partial Test Ban Treaty—PTBT),** *1963*
Number of parties: 112.

Prohibits the carrying out of any nuclear weapon test explosion or any other nuclear explosion: (*a*) in the atmosphere, beyond its limits, including outer space, or under water, including territorial waters or high seas; or (*b*) in any other environment if such explosion causes radioactive debris to be present outside the territorial limits of the state under whose jurisdiction or control the explosion is conducted.

**Treaty on principles governing the activities of states in the exploration and use of outer space, including the Moon and other celestial bodies
(Outer Space Treaty),** *1967*
Number of parties: 85.

Prohibits the placing in orbit around the Earth of any objects carrying nuclear weapons or any other kinds of weapons of mass destruction, the installation of such weapons on celestial bodies, or the stationing of them in outer space in any other manner. The establishment of military bases, installations and fortifications, the testing of any type of weapons and the conduct of military manoeuvres on celestial bodies are also forbidden.

Treaty for the prohibition of nuclear weapons in Latin America (Treaty of Tlatelolco), *1967*
Number of parties: 23.

Prohibits the testing, use, manufacture, production or acquisition by any means, as well as the receipt, storage, installation, deployment and any form of possession of any nuclear weapons by Latin American countries.

The parties should conclude agreements with the IAEA for the application of safeguards to their nuclear activities.

Under *Additional Protocol I*, annexed to the Treaty, the extra-continental or continental states which, *de jure* or *de facto*, are internationally responsible for territories lying within the limits of the geographical zone established by the Treaty (France, the Netherlands, the UK and the USA), undertake to apply the status of military denuclearization, as defined in the Treaty, to such territories.

Under *Additional Protocol II*, annexed to the Treaty, the nuclear weapon states undertake to respect the statute of military denuclearization of Latin America, as defined and delimited in the Treaty, and not to contribute to acts involving a violation of the Treaty, nor to use or threaten to use nuclear weapons against the parties to the Treaty.

Treaty on the non-proliferation of nuclear weapons (NPT), *1968*
Number of parties: 124.

Prohibits the transfer by nuclear weapon states, to any recipient whatsoever, of nuclear weapons or other nuclear explosive devices or of control over them, as well as the assistance, encouragement or inducement of any non-nuclear weapon state to manufacture or otherwise acquire such weapons or devices. Prohibits the receipt by non-nuclear weapon states from any transferor whatsoever, as well as the manufacture or other acquisition by those states, of nuclear weapons or other nuclear explosive devices.

Non-nuclear weapon states undertake to conclude safeguards agreements with the International Atomic Energy Agency (IAEA) with a view to preventing diversion of nuclear energy from peaceful uses to nuclear weapons or other nuclear explosive devices.

The parties undertake to facilitate the exchange of equipment, materials and scientific and technological information for the peaceful uses of nuclear energy and to ensure that potential benefits from peaceful applications of nuclear explosions will be made available to non-nuclear weapon parties to the Treaty. They also undertake to pursue negotiations in good faith on effective measures relating to cessation of the nuclear arms race at an early date and to nuclear disarmament, and on a treaty on general and complete disarmament.

Treaty on the prohibition of the emplacement of nuclear weapons and other weapons of mass destruction on the sea-bed and the ocean floor and in the subsoil thereof (Sea-Bed Treaty), *1971*
Number of parties: 75.

Prohibits emplanting or emplacing on the sea-bed and the ocean floor and in the subsoil thereof beyond the outer limit of a sea-bed zone (coterminous with the 12-mile outer limit of the zone referred to in the 1958 Geneva Convention on the Territorial Sea and the Contiguous Zone) any nuclear weapons or any other types of weapon of mass destruction as well as structures, launching installations or any other facilities specifically designed for storing, testing or using such weapons.

Convention on the prohibition of the development, production and stockpiling of bacteriological (biological) and toxin weapons and on their destruction (BW Convention), *1972*
Number of parties: 101.

Prohibits the development, production, stockpiling or acquisition by other means or retention of microbial or other biological agents, or toxins whatever their origin or method of production, of types and in quantities that have no justification for prophylactic, protective or other peaceful purposes, as well as weapons, equipment or means of delivery designed to use such agents or toxins for hostile purposes or in armed conflict. The destruction of the agents, toxins, weapons, equipment and means of delivery in the possession of the parties, or their diversion to peaceful purposes, should be effected not later than nine months after the entry into force of the Convention.

Document on confidence-building measures and certain aspects of security and disarmament, included in the Final Act of the Conference on Security and Co-operation in Europe (CSCE) (Helsinki Declaration), *1975*
Provides for notification of major military manoeuvres in Europe to be given at least 21 days in advance or, in the case of a manoeuvre arranged at shorter notice, at the earliest possible opportunity prior to its starting date. The term "major" means that at least 25 000 troops are involved. The following information is to be provided: the designation of the manoeuvre (if any); its general purpose; the states involved; the types and the numerical strength of the forces engaged; and the area and estimated timeframe of its conduct. States may invite observers to attend the manoeuvres.

The Final Act was signed by Austria, Belgium, Bulgaria, Canada, Cyprus, Czechoslovakia, Denmark, Finland, France, German Democratic Republic, Federal Republic of Germany, Greece, Holy See, Hungary, Iceland, Ireland, Italy, Liechtenstein, Luxembourg, Malta, Monaco, Netherlands, Norway, Poland, Portugal, Romania, San Marino, Spain, Sweden, Switzerland, Turkey, UK, USA, USSR, Yugoslavia.

Convention on the prohibition of military or any other hostile use of environmental modification techniques (Enmod Convention), *1977*
Number of parties: 47.

Prohibits military or any other hostile use of environmental modification techniques having widespread, long-lasting or severe effects as the means of destruction, damage or injury to states party to the Convention. The term "environmental modification techniques" refers to any technique for changing—through the deliberate manipulation of natural processes—the dynamics, composition or structure of the Earth, including its biota, lithosphere, hydrosphere and atmosphere, or of outer space.

The understandings reached during the negotiations, but not written into the Convention, define the terms "widespread", "long-lasting" and "severe".

Protocol (I) Additional to the 1949 Geneva Conventions and relating to the protection of victims of international armed conflicts, *1977*
Number of parties: 48.

Reiterates the rule of international law that it is prohibited to use weapons and methods of war that cause superfluous injury or unnecessary suffering, and expands the existing prohibition against indiscriminate attacks to cover attacks by bombardment of cities or other areas containing a similar concentration of civilians. Dams, dykes and nuclear electric power generating stations are placed under special protection. Guerrilla fighters are accorded the right to prisoner-of-war status if they belong to organized units subject to an internal disciplinary system and under a command responsible to the party concerned.

Protocol (II) Additional to the 1949 Geneva Conventions and relating to the protection of victims of non-international armed conflicts, *1977*
Number of parties: 41.

Relates to the protection of victims of non-international armed conflicts. It prescribes humane treatment of all the persons involved in such conflicts, care for the wounded, sick and shipwrecked, as well as protection of civilians against the dangers arising from military operations.

Convention on the prohibitions or restrictions on the use of certain conventional weapons which may be deemed to be excessively injurious or to have indiscriminate effects ('Inhumane Weapons' Convention), *1981*
Number of parties: 24.

The Convention is an 'umbrella treaty', under which specific agreements can be concluded in the form of protocols.

Protocol I prohibits the use of weapons intended to injure by fragments which are not detectable in the human body by X-rays.

Protocol II prohibits or restricts the use of mines, booby-traps and similar devices.

Protocol III prohibits or restricts the use of incendiary weapons.

LIST OF PARTIES TO 10 MULTILATERAL TREATIES

The position of some countries in relation to the Treaty of Tlatelolco is complicated. Unlike other parties to the treaty, Brazil and Chile have not waived the requirement that no one at all is to be considered a party until all countries in the region have ratified. There are two protocols annexed to the treaty (see page 103). The Netherlands, the UK and the USA have ratified Protocol I; France has only signed it. The five nuclear weapon powers have ratified Protocol II.

	Geneva Protocol	*Antarctic Treaty*	*Partial Test Ban Treaty*	*Outer Space Treaty*	*Treaty of Tlatelolco*	*Non-Proliferation Treaty*	*Sea-Bed Treaty*	*Biological Weapons Convention*	*Enmod Convention*	*'Inhumane Weapons' Convention*
Afghanistan			✓			✓	✓	✓		
Antigua and Barbuda					✓					
Argentina	✓	✓		✓			✓	✓		
Australia	✓	✓	✓	✓		✓	✓	✓	✓	✓
Austria	✓		✓	✓		✓	✓	✓		✓
Bahamas			✓	✓	✓	✓				
Bangladesh						✓			✓	
Barbados	✓		✓	✓	✓	✓		✓		
Belgium	✓	✓	✓	✓		✓	✓	✓	✓	
Benin			✓			✓		✓		
Bhutan	✓		✓					✓		
Bolivia			✓		✓	✓		✓		
Botswana			✓			✓	✓			
Brazil	✓	✓	✓	✓				✓	✓	
Bulgaria	✓		✓	✓		✓	✓	✓	✓	✓
Burkina Faso (formerly Upper Volta)	✓			✓		✓				
Burma			✓			✓				
Burundi						✓				
Byelorussia	✓		✓	✓		✓	✓	✓	✓	✓

	Geneva Protocol	Antarctic Treaty	Partial Test Ban Treaty	Outer Space Treaty	Treaty of Tlatelolco	Non-Proliferation Treaty	Sea-Bed Treaty	Biological Weapons Convention	Enmod Convention	Inhumane Weapons' Convention
Cameroon						✓				
Canada	✓		✓	✓		✓	✓	✓	✓	
Cape Verde				✓		✓	✓	✓	✓	
Central African Republic	✓		✓			✓	✓			
Chad			✓			✓				
Chile	✓	✓	✓	✓				✓		
China	✓	✓		✓				✓		✓
Colombia					✓			✓		
Congo						✓	✓	✓		
Costa Rica			✓		✓	✓				
Cuba	✓	✓		✓			✓	✓	✓	
Cyprus	✓		✓	✓		✓	✓	✓	✓	
Czechoslovakia	✓	✓	✓	✓		✓	✓	✓	✓	✓
Denmark	✓	✓	✓	✓		✓	✓	✓	✓	✓
Dominica										
Dominican Republic	✓		✓	✓	✓	✓		✓		
Ecuador	✓		✓	✓	✓	✓		✓		✓
Egypt	✓		✓	✓		✓			✓	
El Salvador			✓	✓	✓	✓				
Equatorial Guinea						✓				
Ethiopia	✓					✓	✓	✓		
Fiji	✓		✓	✓		✓				
Finland	✓	✓	✓	✓		✓	✓	✓	✓	✓
France	✓	✓		✓				✓		
Gabon			✓			✓				
Gambia	✓		✓							
Germany, East	✓	✓	✓	✓		✓	✓	✓	✓	✓
Germany, West	✓	✓	✓	✓		✓	✓	✓	✓	
Ghana	✓		✓			✓	✓	✓	✓	
Greece	✓		✓	✓		✓		✓	✓	
Grenada					✓					
Guatemala	✓		✓		✓	✓		✓		✓
Guinea-Bissau			✓	✓			✓	✓		
Haiti					✓	✓				
Holy See (Vatican City)	✓					✓				
Honduras			✓		✓	✓		✓		
Hungary	✓	✓	✓	✓		✓	✓	✓	✓	✓
Iceland	✓		✓	✓		✓	✓	✓		
India	✓	✓	✓	✓			✓	✓	✓	✓
Indonesia	✓		✓			✓				
Iran	✓		✓			✓	✓	✓		
Iraq	✓		✓	✓		✓	✓			
Ireland	✓		✓	✓		✓	✓	✓	✓	
Israel	✓		✓	✓						
Italy	✓	✓	✓	✓		✓	✓	✓	✓	
Ivory Coast	✓		✓			✓				
Jamaica	✓			✓	✓	✓		✓		
Japan	✓	✓	✓	✓		✓	✓	✓	✓	✓
Jordan	✓		✓			✓	✓	✓		
Kampuchea	✓					✓				

	Geneva Protocol	Antarctic Treaty	Partial Test Ban Treaty	Outer Space Treaty	Treaty of Tlatelolco	Non-Proliferation Treaty	Sea-Bed Treaty	Biological Weapons Convention	Enmod Convention	'Inhumane Weapons' Convention
Kenya	✓		✓			✓		✓		
Korea, North						✓			✓	
Korea, South			✓	✓		✓				
Kuwait	✓		✓	✓				✓		✓
Lao People's Dem. Rep.			✓	✓		✓	✓	✓	✓	✓
Lebanon	✓		✓	✓		✓		✓		
Lesotho	✓					✓	✓	✓		
Liberia	✓		✓			✓				
Libya	✓		✓	✓		✓		✓		
Liechtenstein						✓				
Luxembourg	✓		✓			✓		✓		
Madagascar	✓		✓	✓		✓				
Malawi	✓		✓						✓	
Malaysia	✓		✓			✓	✓			
Maldives	✓					✓				
Mali				✓		✓				
Malta	✓		✓			✓	✓	✓		
Mauritania			✓							
Mauritius	✓		✓	✓		✓	✓	✓		
Mexico	✓		✓	✓	✓	✓	✓	✓		✓
Monaco	✓									
Mongolia	✓		✓	✓		✓	✓	✓	✓	✓
Morocco	✓		✓	✓		✓	✓			
Nauru						✓				
Nepal	✓		✓	✓		✓	✓			
Netherlands	✓	✓	✓	✓		✓	✓	✓	✓	
New Zealand	✓	✓	✓	✓		✓	✓	✓	✓	
Nicaragua			✓		✓	✓	✓	✓		
Niger	✓		✓	✓		✓	✓	✓		
Nigeria	✓		✓	✓		✓		✓		
Norway	✓	✓	✓	✓		✓	✓	✓	✓	✓
Pakistan	✓		✓	✓				✓		
Panama	✓		✓		✓	✓		✓		
Papua New Guinea	✓	✓	✓	✓		✓			✓	
Paraguay	✓				✓	✓		✓		
Peru		✓	✓	✓	✓	✓				
Philippines	✓		✓			✓		✓		
Poland	✓	✓	✓	✓		✓	✓	✓	✓	✓
Portugal	✓					✓	✓	✓		
Qatar	✓						✓	✓		
Romania	✓	✓	✓	✓		✓	✓	✓	✓	
Rwanda	✓		✓			✓	✓	✓		
Saint Lucia						✓				
Saint Vincent						✓				
Samoa			✓			✓				
San Marino			✓	✓		✓		✓		
Sao Tome and Principe						✓	✓	✓		
Saudi Arabia	✓			✓			✓	✓		
Senegal	✓		✓			✓				
Seychelles				✓		✓	✓	✓		
Sierra Leone	✓		✓	✓		✓		✓		
Singapore			✓	✓		✓	✓			

	Geneva Protocol	Antarctic Treaty	Partial Test Ban Treaty	Outer Space Treaty	Treaty of Tlatelolco	Non-Proliferation Treaty	Sea-Bed Treaty	Biological Weapons Convention	Enmod Convention	Inhumane Weapons' Convention
Solomon Islands						✓	✓	✓	✓	
Somalia						✓				
South Africa	✓	✓	✓	✓		·	✓	✓		
Spain	✓	✓	✓	✓				✓	✓	
Sri Lanka	✓		✓			✓			✓	
Sudan	✓		✓			✓				
Suriname					✓	✓				
Swaziland			✓			✓	✓			
Sweden	✓	✓	✓	✓		✓	✓	✓	✓	✓
Switzerland	✓		✓	✓		✓	✓	✓		✓
Syria	✓		✓	✓		✓				
Taiwan	✓		✓	✓		✓	✓	✓		
Tanzania	✓		✓							
Thailand	✓		✓	✓		✓		✓		
Togo	✓		✓			✓	✓	✓		
Tonga	✓		✓	✓		✓	✓	✓		
Trinidad and Tobago	✓		✓		✓					
Tunisia	✓		✓	✓		✓	✓	✓	✓	
Turkey	✓		✓	✓		✓	✓			
Tuvalu						✓				
Uganda	✓		✓	✓		✓				
UK	✓	✓	✓	✓		✓	✓	✓	✓	
Ukraine			✓	✓			✓	✓	✓	✓
Uruguay	✓	✓	✓	✓	✓	✓				
USA	✓	✓	✓	✓		✓	✓	✓	✓	
USSR	✓	✓	✓	✓		✓	✓	✓	✓	✓
Venezuela	✓		✓	✓	✓	✓				
Viet Nam	✓			✓		✓	✓	✓	✓	
Yemen Arab Republic	✓								✓	
Yemen, People's Dem. Rep.			✓	✓		✓	✓	✓	✓	
Yugoslavia	✓		✓	✓		✓	✓	✓		✓
Zaire			✓			✓		✓		
Zambia			✓	✓			✓			

Index

Treaties will be found grouped together under Disarmament and arms control treaties and agreements.

Abbreviations, 86
ABMs (anti-ballistic missile systems):
  ASAT and, 19
  definition, 9
  USSR's, 41, 46, 50, 90
  See also ABM Treaty *under* SALT I *and for new US system see* Star Wars
Afghanistan, 51, 56, 73
Africa:
  arms imports, 71, 99
  military expenditure, 59, 97, 100
Agent Orange, 58
Aircraft:
  France, 39, 94
  international:
    European Fighter Aircraft, 64
    Tornado, 38, 39, 63, 94
  UK, 39, 63, 94
  USA:
    bombers, 7, 32, 33, 34, 35, 40, 61, 89, 90
    fighters, 35, 43, 44, 61, 72, 75
  USSR:
    bombers, 33, 37, 89, 91, 92
    fighters, 70, 75
  see also Helicopters
Aircraft-carriers, 40, 66
Ammunition, 11
Anthrax, 56
Argentina, 23, 75
Arms control *see* Disarmament and arms control
Arms production, 13, 15, 64, 74
Arms trade:
  suppliers, 70–4, 101
  trends, 13–15, 69, 74–6
  volume of, 14
Artillery, nuclear, 35
ASAT (anti-satellite activity), 41, 42–4, 48, 49:
  ABMs and, 19, 48, 49–50
ASW (anti-submarine warfare) systems, 90, 91
Australia, 22
Austria, 28

B-1 bomber, 34, 61, 92
B-52 bomber, 7, 35, 40, 89, 92
Backfire bomber, 89, 92
Balkans, 22
Ballistic missile defence *see* ABMs, Star Wars
Battlefield nuclear weapons, 1
Beam weapons, 3 *see also* Lasers
Belgium, 29, 35, 74
Binary munitions, 52, 53
Biological weapons, 56–8
Bombs, nuclear, 35, 38, 39, 93
Brazil, 13, 23, 58, 69
Bridges, 11
Buccaneer aircraft, 39, 94

Burma, 56
Burt, Richard, 36

C^3I (command, control, communications and intelligence), 5, 8, 82
Canada, 62–3, 74
Carter, President Jimmy (James Earl Jr), 71
Central America:
  arms imports, 71
  military expenditure, 67, 97, 100
Chemical weapons, 51–6, 96
Chernenko, President Konstantin, 64
Chevaline warhead, 38
China:
  arms exports, 71, 72, 101
  arms imports, 72
  chemical weapons, 56
  disarmament issues and, 20
  military expenditure, 59, 66–7, 97, 100
  nuclear explosions, 21, 95
  nuclear forces, 39, 94
  US naval vessels and, 28
Cluster bombs, 54
Coffee brewer, expensive, 61
Conference on Disarmament, 19–20, 51
Confidence-building measures, 11
Costa Rica, 67
Cruise missiles *see* Missiles, cruise
Cuba, 56
Cyprus, 22
Czechoslovakia, 18, 31, 38, 70

Deng Xiaoping, 67
Destabilization, 11, 44, 48, 82
Deterrence, 9, 36
Disarmament and arms control:
  chemical weapons, 19
  comprehensive test ban treaty, 20
  Europe, force reductions in, 20
  force, non-use of, 21
  nuclear weapons:
    Geneva talks on, 1, 16–19, 61, 77–84
    no-first-use, 21–2
    suggestions for, 6, 80–4
  prospects for, 16–29
  space weapons, 16, 19
  see also following entry
Disarmament and arms control treaties and agreements:
  Antarctic Treaty 1959, 102, 107–10
  Biological Weapons Convention 1972, 51, 56, 105, 107–10
  Enmod Convention 1977, 106, 107–10
  Geneva Conventions 1949, 102, 106

Geneva Protocol 1925, 51, 52, 56, 102, 107–10
Helsinki Declaration 1975, 105
'Inhumane Weapons' Convention 1981, 107–10
NPT (Non-Proliferation Treaty) 1968, 22–3, 78, 104, 107–10
Outer Space Treaty 1967, 103, 107–10
Partial Test Ban Treaty 1963, 20, 21, 103, 107–10
Sea-Bed Treaty 1971, 104, 107–10
Tlatelolco Treaty 1967, 103, 107–10
see also SALT Treaties

Economic recession, 11, 13, 69, 74
Egypt, 13, 56, 67–8, 69, 72, 73
Electronics, 66
El Salvador, 67
EMP warhead, 5
ET (emerging technology), 3, 9–11
Ethiopia, 56
Europe:
  chemical weapon-free zone, 22
  Conference on Security and Co-operation, 21–2
  military expenditure, 59, 62, 97, 100
  missiles in:
    USA, 1, 7, 18, 29, 31, 35, 77, 82, 93
    USSR, 18, 31, 38, 82
Exocet missiles, 75, 76

F-15 aircraft, 43, 44, 72
F-16 aircraft, 35, 61, 72, 75
Falklands/Malvinas War, 63, 67, 75
Far East:
  arms imports, 71, 99
  military expenditure, 59, 67, 97, 100
FB-111, 89
Fiji, 28
Finland, 22, 38
First strike, 8, 18, 31, 83
France:
  arms exports, 69, 73, 75, 76, 101
  arms production, 64
  chemical weapons, 53
  disarmament issues and, 20
  modernization programme, 64
  nuclear explosions, 21, 95
  nuclear forces, x, 18, 38, 39, 64, 94
  public opinion, 24

German Democratic Republic, 18, 31, 38, 76
Germany, Federal Republic of:
  aircraft in, 38
  arms exports, 69, 73, 74, 101
  arms production, 64

111

chemical weapons, 52-3
missiles in, 7, 29, 31, 35, 82
public opinion, 24, 29
Gorbachev, President M.S., 38, 79
Greece, 72
Gromyko, Andrei, 16
Guatemala, 67

Helicopters, 61, 64
Helsinki Conference, 21
Honduras, 67, 75
Howitzer shells, 53, 72
Hubner, J., 54

Iceland, 28
India, 23, 56, 58, 67, 69, 70, 95
Indonesia, 13
Iran:
  arms imports, 73, 74
  Iraq, war with, 15, 52, 55-6, 68, 76
  military expenditure, 67
Iraq:
  arms imports, 69, 70, 73
  chemical weapons used by, 52, 55-6
  Iran, war with, 15, 52, 55-6, 68, 76
  military expenditure, 67
Israel, 23, 56, 68, 69
Italy:
  arms exports, 69, 73, 76, 101
  arms production, 64
  Comiso, 35
  military expenditure, 62
  missiles in, 35
  modernization programme, 63
  public opinion, 24, 29

Jaguar aircraft, 39, 94
Japan, 20, 24, 67
Jordan, 70, 75

Kalashnikov rifles, 73
Kampuchea, 68
Kaplan, Fred, 54
Kinetic energy weapons, 45
Korea, North, 56, 71, 75
Korea, South, 13, 73, 75
Kuwait, 70, 75

Lance missile, 35, 90, 93
Lasers, 5, 45
Latin America:
  arms imports, 71, 99
  military expenditure, 59
Launch on warning, 8-9, 82
Libya, 56, 69
Liechtenstein, 22
LOCPODs (low-cost powered dispensers), 10
M-1 battle tank, 61
MAD (mutual assured destruction), 45
Malta, 22
Microtechnology, 9
Middle East:
  arms imports, 71, 73, 99
  military expenditure, 59, 67, 97, 100

Midgetman missile, 34, 92
MiG aircraft, 70, 75
Military expenditure:
  annual rates of change, 100
  resources consumed by, 13
  table, summary, 97
  trends, 11-13, 59-68
  see also following entry
Military expenditure on research and development, 4, 11, 58, 61, 66
Military manoeuvres, notification of, 21
Mines, land, 53
Minuteman missile, 33, 50, 89
Mirage aircraft, 39, 94
MIRVs (multiple independently targetable re-entry vehicles), 7, 31, 37, 38, 45
Missiles, ballistic:
  general references
  accuracy, 7, 33, 37
  chemical weapons, 54
  flight time, 8, 31, 33, 82
  ranges, 7
  silos, 7, 47
  solid-fuelled, 7
  throw-weight, 35
  individual countries
  China, 39, 94
  France, 39, 94
  UK, 18, 38, 63, 94
  USA:
    ICBMs (intercontinental ballistic missiles), 7, 32, 33, 50, 89, 92
    theatre nuclear, 7, 31, 33, 35, 90, 92, 93
    SLBMs (submarine-launched ballistic missiles), 32, 33, 34-5, 89, 92, 93
  USSR:
    ICBMs (intercontinental ballistic missiles), 33, 36
    theatre nuclear, 18-19, 33, 37, 38, 89, 91
    SLBMs (submarine-launched ballistic missiles), 33, 36-7
Missiles, cruise:
  general references
  arms control and, 40
  chemical weapons and, 53
  deployment, 31
  operation of, 8
  significance, 7-9, 31
  individual countries
  USA:
    ALCMs (air-launched cruise missiles), 7, 32, 35, 40, 92
    GLCMs (ground-launched cruise missiles), 1, 35, 38, 90, 92, 93
    SLCMs (sea-launched cruise missiles), 3, 7, 35, 39-40, 90, 92
  USSR, 38, 39
MLRS (multiple launch rocket system), 10, 53
Mustard gas, 55
MX missile, 7, 28, 32, 34, 61, 80, 92

NATO (North Atlantic Treaty Organization):
  arms exports, 69
  chemical weapons, 51, 52-3, 54
  consensus broken, 77
  disarmament issues and, 21, 22
  ET weapons and, 3
  Long Term Defence programme, 62
  military expenditure, 11, 12, 59, 62-5, 97, 100
  nuclear weapons, reliance on, 62
  Warsaw Pact, weapon systems different from, 6
Nerve gas, 51, 52, 53
Netherlands, 24, 29, 37
Neutron bomb, 5
New Zealand, 28
Nicaragua, 67, 75
Nigeria, 70
Nimrod Airborne Early Warning aircraft, 63
North Atlantic Treaty Organization see NATO
Norway, 24, 38
Nuclear energy, 23
Nuclear explosions, 21, 95
Nuclear war: nuclear winter, 25-8
Nuclear weapons:
  accuracy, 3, 6, 31, 33
  expansion, 1, 6-7
  hostility to, 28-9
  modernization, 1, 32, 34, 35
  new roles for, 31
  new types, 5
  numbers of, 3, 6, 31, 33, 34-6 passim, 38, 88-94

Oceania, 59, 97, 100

Pakistan, 23, 56, 72, 73
Papua New Guinea, 28
Patriot air defence missile system, 61
'Peacekeeper' missile see MX missile
Pershing II missile, 1, 7, 31, 33, 35, 38, 53, 82, 90, 92, 93
Peru, 56, 67
PLO (Palestine Liberation Organization), 56
Polaris submarines, 38, 63
Poseidon missile, 89, 93
Poseidon submarine, 34
Public opinion, 1, 23-5, 77-8

Radar, 50
Railguns, 45
Reagan, President Ronald, 9, 16, 20, 32, 34, 35, 45, 50, 52, 53, 54, 60, 71
Research and development, 4 see also Military expenditure on research and development, Technology
Rocket motors, 36
Rogers, General Bernard, 52, 62
Romania, 70
Russia see Union of Soviet Socialist Republics

112

SALT I:
    ABM Treaty 1972, 49–50, 78, 81
    Interim Agreement 1972, 78
SALT II, 6, 50, 78, 81
San Marino, 22
Satellites, 41, 42, 49 see also ASAT
Saudi Arabia, 69, 72, 73
Scowcroft Commission, 17–18
SDI see Star Wars
Second strike, 9
Ships: production of, 64, 66
South Africa, 23
South America:
    military expenditure, 67, 97, 100
South Asia:
    arms imports, 71, 99
    military expenditure, 59, 67, 97, 100
South Pacific Forum, 28
Soviet Union see Union of Soviet Socialist Republics
Space: militarization of, 1 see also following entry, ASAT satellites, Star Wars
Space weapons, 412–50:
    arms control implications, 41, 49–50
    see also ASAT, Satellites, Star Wars
Spain, 24, 64
SS-4, 18, 91
SS-5, 18
SS-12, 31, 38, 82
SS-19, 33
SS-20, 18, 37, 38, 89, 91
SS-22, 31, 33, 38, 82
Stalin, Josef, 53
Star Wars, 9, 31, 37, 41, 45–9, 83:
    arms control and, 9, 16, 41, 49–50, 81, 82
'Stealth' technology, 5
Stinger missile, 70
Stockholm Conference, 21–2
Strategic Defense Initiative see Star Wars
Submarines:
    UK, 38, 63
    USA, 18, 34–5, 40, 92
    USSR, 7, 37, 38
Super Etendard aircraft, 39, 94
SWAPO (South West African People's Liberation Army), 56
Sweden, 22, 73
Switzerland, 22, 73
Syria, 69, 70

T-72 tank, 66
T-74/T-80 tank, 65

Tactical nuclear weapons, 1
Taiwan, 72, 73
Tanks, 11, 61, 65, 66
Technology:
    arms control and, 5, 6
    arms race fuelled by, 3–6, 36
Thailand, 75
Theatre nuclear forces see Missiles, ballistic
Third World:
    arms exports, 101
    arms imports, 13, 14, 69, 70, 98, 99
    arms production, 13
    debts, 11, 13
    military expenditure, 11, 13
Thor missile, 42
Threats, perception of, 17–18, 32, 36, 40, 48, 62
Titan missile, 89
Tomahawk missile, 35, 40, 90
Tornado aircraft, 38, 39, 63, 94
Trident missile, 34–5, 38, 63, 82, 89, 92
Trident submarine, 34, 61, 63, 92
Turkey, 72
Typhoon submarine, 37

Union of Soviet Socialist Republics:
    arms exports, 67, 69, 70, 76, 98, 101
    biological weapons allegations against, 56–7
    chemical weapons, 51, 54–5, 96
    chemical weapons use alleged, 51
    disarmament issues and, 1, 16, 17, 18, 19–20, 23, 44
    inferiority, sense of, 31
    military expenditure, 64–6, 97, 100
    Moscow, 7, 8
    Navy, 38
    nuclear explosions, 21, 95
    nuclear forces, x, 6–7, 31, 32, 33, 35–8, 89, 91, 92
    Sverdlovsk, 56
    USA, relations with, 1, 6, 77
United Kingdom:
    arms exports, 73, 74, 75, 101
    arms production, 64
    chemical weapons and, 52–3
    cruise missiles in, 1
    disarmament issues and, 23
    Greenham Common, 35
    military expenditure, 62, 63–4
    missiles (USA's) in, 35
    nuclear explosions, 95
    nuclear forces, x, 18, 38–9, 63, 94
    public opinion, 24, 29

United Nations, 52, 54, 56
United States of America:
    Air Force, 61, 62
    arms exports, 69, 71–3, 75, 76, 98, 101
    arms production, 64–5
    Army, 62
    battle readiness, 62
    biological weapons allegations against, 56
    chemical weapons, 51, 52, 53, 96
    CIA, 54, 56
    Congress, 52, 54, 60, 61, 62, 80
    disarmament issues and, 1, 16, 17, 18, 19–20, 23, 44, 61
    Iran, hostages in, 60
    Lawrence Livermore Laboratory, 4, 5
    Los Alamos Laboratory, 4
    military aid given by, 67, 68
    military expenditure, 11, 34, 59, 60–2, 97, 100
    Navy, 3, 7, 34, 62
    nuclear explosions, 21, 95
    nuclear forces, x, 7, 31, 32–5, 89, 90, 92
    public opinion, 23, 24, 29, 36, 60, 61
    rearmament programme, 11, 59, 60, 77, 82–3
    USSR, relations with, 1, 6, 77
    Viet Nam War and, 58

Viet Nam, 56, 57, 68

War fighting strategies, 36, 39
Warsaw Pact:
    arms exports, 69, 70
    chemical weapons, 51, 54
    disarmament issues and, 21
    Europe, troop numbers in, 20
    military expenditure, 11, 12, 59, 97, 100
    NATO, weapon systems different from, 6

X-ray laser, 5

Yellow Rain, 57
Yemen, South, 69
Yugoslavia, 22, 70

113

World Armaments and Disarmament, SIPRI Yearbook 1985

Contents List

Introduction
FRANK BLACKABY
Appendix A. Public Opinion
EYMERT DEN OUDSTEN

Chapter 1. Nuclear weapons
WILLIAM M. ARKIN, ANDREW S. BURROWS,
RICHARD W. FIELDHOUSE, THOMAS B. COCHRAN,
ROBERT S. NORRIS and JEFFREY I. SANDS

Chapter 2. Nuclear explosions
RAGNHILD FERM
Appendix 2A. Nuclear explosions, 1983 (revised data for the USA) and 1984 (preliminary data)
Appendix 2B. Nuclear explosions, 1945–84 (known and presumed)

Chapter 3. Third-generation nuclear weapons
KOSTA TSIPIS
Appendix 3A. The X-ray laser

Chapter 4. Global consequences of a nuclear war: a review of recent Soviet studies
A. S. GINSBURG, G. S. GOLITSYN and A. A. VASILIEV
Appendix 4A. Nuclear winter: a bibliography
ARTHUR H. WESTING

Chapter 5. The military use of outer space
BHUPENDRA JASANI and G. E. PERRY
Appendix 5A. Space weapons
Appendix 5B. Tables of satellites launched in 1984

Chapter 6. Chemical and biological warfare: developments in 1984
J. P. PERRY ROBINSON
Appendix 6A. An analysis of the reports of Iraqi chemical warfare against Iran, 1980–84

Chapter 7. World military expenditure and arms production
MICHAEL BRZOSKA, GERD HAGMEYER-GAVERUS, EVAMARIA LOOSE-WEINTRAUB, ELISABETH SKÖNS, RITA TULLBERG and GORDON ADAMS
Appendix 7A. Tables of world military expenditure, 1975–84

Chapter 8. Military research and development expenditure
MARY ACLAND-HOOD

Chapter 9. Militarization in Africa
ROBIN LUCKHAM
Appendix 9A. Inventory of military government, armed conflict and external military intervention in post-colonial Africa

Chapter 10. Arms production in the Third World
HERBERT WULF

Chapter 11. The trade in major conventional weapons
MICHAEL BRZOSKA and THOMAS OHLSON
Appendix 11A. Aggregate tables of the value of the trade in major weapons with the Third World, 1965–84
Appendix 11B. Register of the trade in major conventional weapons with industrialized and Third World countries, 1984
Appendix 11C. Register of licensed production of major conventional weapons in industrialized and Third World countries, 1984
Appendix 11D. Criteria, values and conventions

Chapter 12. Military-related debt in non-oil developing countries, 1972–82
RITA TULLBERG
Appendix 12A. Definitions and methods

Chapter 13. Multilateral arms control efforts
JOZEF GOLDBLAT
Appendix 13A. UN General Assembly resolutions and decisions on disarmament, 1984

Chapter 14. Major multilateral arms control agreements
JOZEF GOLDBLAT and RAGNHILD FERM

Chapter 15. The first year of the Stockholm Conference
KARL E. BIRNBAUM
Appendix 15A. Notification of military manoeuvres in 1984, in compliance with the Final Act of the CSCE

Chapter 16. The Sinai peacekeeping experience: a verification paradigm for Europe
DAVID BARTON
Appendix 16A. Second Sinai Disengagement Agreement, Egypt and Israel, September 1, 1975
Appendix 16B. Treaty of Peace between the Arab Republic of Egypt and the State of Israel

Chapter 17. The conflict in Afghanistan
JEAN-CHRISTOPHE VICTOR
Appendix 17A. Treaty of Friendship, Goodneighbourliness and Cooperation between the U.S.S.R. and the Democratic Republic of Afghanistan, 5 December 1978
Appendix 17B. UN General Assembly resolution 39/13: The situation in Afghanistan and its implications for international peace and security, 21 November 1984

Chapter 18. Conscientious objection to military service
PETER WHITTLE
Appendix 18A. The recognition of conscientious objection
Appendix 18B. Document of international bodies ruling on conscientious objection

Chronology of major events related to arms control issues
JOZEF GOLDBLAT and RAGNHILD FERM

For Product Safety Concerns and Information please contact our EU
representative GPSR@taylorandfrancis.com
Taylor & Francis Verlag GmbH, Kaufingerstraße 24, 80331 München, Germany

www.ingramcontent.com/pod-product-compliance
Lightning Source LLC
Chambersburg PA
CBHW081831300426
44116CB00014B/2554